THE
NATURAL
DEPTH IN MAN

WILSON VAN DUSEN

THE NATURAL DEPTH IN MAN

SWEDENBORG FOUNDATION, INC.
NEW YORK

Acknowledgment is made for permission to quote from copyrighted materials as follows:

Article "Self-Reflection in the Forging of a Person" by Wilson Van Dusen, from *Experiences in Being* by Bernice Marshall. © 1971 by Wadsworth Publishing Company, Inc., Belmont, California 94002. Reprinted by permission of the publishers, Brooks/Cole Publishing Company.

Lines from "Little Gidding" in *Four Quartets*, copyright, 1943, by T.S. Eliot; renewed, 1971, by Esme Valerie Eliot. Reprinted by permission of Harcourt Brace Jovanovich, Inc., and Faber and Faber, Ltd.

First Printing 1972 Harper & Row, N.Y., NY
Second Printing 1981 Swedenborg Foundation
139 East 23rd Street
New York, NY 10010
Library of Congress Catalog Card Number 72-78055
ISBN 0-87785-165-4
Cover design by Nancy Crompton

To my teacher, Father Raymond Henry Shevenell, School
of Psychology, University of Ottawa, Ottawa, Canada

Contents

1

The Castle of the Mind

And the end of all our exploring
Will be to arrive where we started
And know the place for the first time.
Through the unknown, remembered gate
When the last of earth left to discover
Is that which was the beginning;
At the source of the longest river
The voice of the hidden waterfall
And the children in the apple tree
Not known, because not looked for
But heard, half heard, in the stillness
Between two waves of the sea.
                    T. S. Eliot, "Little Gidding"

If one were locked up in an ancient castle for one's whole life
—a castle full of artifacts, dungeons, endless rooms, art, and
books—one would spend much time exploring and recreating
the lives of the inhabitants. We are locked up in such a mind-
castle, yet we have explored little. Many know little more than
a sitting room in the east wing and assume this is the whole. The

size of the mind-castle is little appreciated. It includes all you have experienced, are experiencing, will experience, and in the remote corners, all you can experience.

We will wander through the domain of the psyche, poking into nooks and crannies, learning and using what we can. The spirit of this wandering is casual, playful. To understand the life of the tenants of the mind-castle we wander from room to room, poke into cupboards, open drawers, look at their books and belongings, and gradually form an impression of the kind of life lived here. This is done respectfully, without wishing to change or disturb the scene. It is done out of curiosity, for fun, and to learn of lives. With rare luck, we may meet the tenant, the one who arranged this scene as it is.

In this wandering through the psyche, the home, and indeed the being of man, I would like to look at a whole range of things, from the simple how it feels to have a face, to the more exotic areas of dreams, fantasies, madness, and mystical experiences. As we shall see, in many ways it is the simple and ordinary aspects of the psyche that are understood least. Exactly how do thoughts and words form? How I move my finger remains something of a mystery to me. It is this naïve, childlike readiness to be surprised that opens out a whole world of possibilities that we normally overlook. For instance, when we enter the hypnogogic state (between sleep and waking) we watch thought and speech form around more primordial feelings that arise within, unbidden and unexpected.

In this there is no effort to be comprehensive or exact. Exactness is hardly possible here. Our purpose is to learn of lives, and to do this we need to be more human than scientific or exact.

Beneath this playful meandering are several more serious implications. For one, I doubt that any single moment of human experience has ever been fully understood or described. In fact, other than the surface wordy aspect of ourselves, most people have only a glimmering of what goes on in their heads. Often

2

their most common fantasy or fear is just half known, and is well hidden from the gaze of others. Nightly we dream several dreams that are marvelously accurate representations of one's life. Most are forgotten. Few can make use of dreams that are recalled. We slip in and out of common fantasies. Words, phrases, and images flit through our head as we go about the day's work. Most of this is lost. We fashion meanings without knowing it. We people the world with our psyche, changing the shape and nature of all and sundry without knowing it. We cannot remember valuable observations of friends about us. Our body has a whole language of its own, pointing to our attitudes, tendencies, and dispositions. This is mostly unnoticed. If we just try to describe all that is in a single moment, we will find it trails off in all directions. We seem mostly unconscious, like wordy fools, barely able to remember what we have said, and with almost no idea how words themselves arise. All this is to say that it is amazing how little of human experience is actually known. We seem to know far more of rocks, clouds, and machines than we do of our own experiencing.

The psyche is constantly generating a vast amount of sensations, images, feelings, half-born ideas, and the like. If this were all set down it would read like an impenetrable rambling. Actually there are remarkable consistencies and even lawfulness in the psyche's operations. This cheers me greatly, for it implies one can make sense out of our hodgepodge selves. It also provides the great challenge of finding the clarifying consistency.

Underlying our playful meandering there is a serious search for the persistent, lawful, or natural in man. These lawful consistencies are like the rock or foundation of our experience. Regardless of what we would like to believe, have been erroneously taught, or theorize, these consistent trends remain as they are. Dreams represent your situation in a symbolic form regardless of whether you care or not, notice them or not, believe in symbolism, or have any ability to use them. Fortunately these inner consistencies run in a single direction. *The most profound tendency of the psyche is to represent itself.* The meaning of this will become clearer as our wandering goes on. This self-representation means that we are almost overburdened with clues about our own nature. It is to me almost unbelievable that all persons can't understand their own dreams, divine their moods by fantasies, capture their attitudes in bodily feelings, and generally confront and understand themselves at every turn. That in the twentieth century one can describe events in common experiences such as the hypnogogic state and surprise people with its structure and contents seems almost beyond belief. Everyone has spent hundreds of hours in this state between sleeping and waking, yet it is largely unknown, but there it is. Our attention seems captured elsewhere by television, our labor, and the many things of the world. Of course the pervasive psyche sneaks out there too, shaping the meanings we find in the world.

What is natural in man is almost an unknown issue in psychology. By natural I mean those consistent realities of our experience that transcend our manipulations. Dreams are symbolic representations of our lives. This symbolizing is natural. The dream can barely speak in any other way. It will do so several times a night regardless of our hopes, fears, education, will power, or belief. These natural tendencies or directions within point beyond our limited understanding to realities we are embedded in. Indeed, our natural tendencies make us.

The whole issue of what is natural in us has almost been abandoned after much debate. We are such collections, such a baggage of education, experiences, reflections of our society, and self-opinions that what is natural, native, or given in ourselves is obscure. It is a doubtful art even to find it.

Years ago, as a clinical psychologist I was assigned to perform psychotherapy on a ward full of women many of whom had been involved in psychotic crimes. I was working with a woman who had written bad checks and appeared so difficult and disturbed in court that she was adjudged mentally ill and sent to a mental hospital. She was difficult in the hospital too. Though in her early forties, she dressed and acted like a seductive teenager. She was an exhibitionist and caught too much of staff attention. It did no good to point out her exhibitionism. She simply could not see it. One day she presented a dream of an Egyptian cat doing a ritualistic dance. Something in her movements caught my eye, for I could see the cat as she told the dream. I asked her to enact the role of the cat. Instantly she was on the floor going through impressive sinuous gyrations. What impressed me was the skill and quality of the movements. I asked if she had ever thought of going into dancing. She had, but wasn't sure she could do it well. A year after she was discharged from the hospital I ran into her in a store. She was making a good living as a teacher of expressive movement. The dream, and my surprised reaction to it, had been the turning point. This annoying exhibitionistic woman wanted to move gracefully before others and be seen by them. This was her nature. Unrecognized and unused by her, her nature intruded anyway as the exhibitionistic patient. Recognized, used, cultivated by her, it became positive and useful both to her and others she worked with.

After that I tried to find the natural drift of the people I met. But it wasn't always easy to find. I recall the son of a psychologist and an artistic mother. This four-year-old boy had a natural interest in all things mechanical. He could work a lock for hours, but he also had to take it apart to see all the fascinating inner workings. I recall women whose pinnacle of fulfillment in their life seemed to be the bearing of children. There are some whose love of words reflects in a kind of tasty savoring of words. I've startled a few of these people at parties when I go up to a stranger and ask if he is a writer, often to find I'd guessed correctly. Similarly the speech of lawyers seems to reflect a kind of enjoyment of the clear ordering of thought. I've long suspected that in the subtle aspects of voice and gesture one could see the underlying nature of the person. The feminine gesture has a round soft expressive quality. Its femininity shows in its tiniest aspects. The male gesture is a less graceful thrust that acts and takes a position. Perhaps the given nature or disposition is the underlying consistency that colors everything a person does.

In the eighteenth century the mystic Emanuel Swedenborg spoke of a ruling love that conditioned all aspects of a person including gestures.

A man's very life is his love, and such as the love is, such is the life, yea, such is the whole man: but it is the ruling or reigning love that constitutes the man. This love holds in subordination many loves (or feelings), which are derivations; these loves appear under a different form, but still are contained in the ruling love, and together with it constitute one kingdom. The ruling love is like their king and head; it directs them, and through them, . . . intends its own end, which is the chief and ultimate end of all the loves. . . .

What a man loves above all things is constantly present in his thought, and also in his will, and it constitutes his veriest life. For example, he who loves wealth above all things, whether it be money or possessions, constantly turns over in his mind how he may attain it: when he does attain it, he rejoices inwardly, when he loses it, he grieves inwardly; for his heart is in it. He who loves himself above all things, remembers himself in everything; he thinks of himself, speaks of himself, acts for the sake of himself; for his life is a life for self.

A man has for an end what he loves above all things, and has respect to it in each and all things; it is in his will, like the hidden current of a stream which draws and bears him away even when busy with something else; for it is that which animates him. This is what one man seeks for, and also sees, in another; and according to which he either leads him or acts with him.

The New Jerusalem (¶54–56), 1758

These natural persistent tendencies of mind are the points at which the individual's conscious self-direction is transcended.

Though the dream is ours, it conceives and speaks in a language somewhat alien to us and in fact cleverer. These points in which we are transcended point beyond ourselves. Indeed, it is fortunate that nature sets these bounds on our experience. If we could fashion ourselves to be whatever we wanted, we would be dreadfully lost. Our conceptions are so limited and based on limited experience. Then, too, it might be hard to make up our minds how we would design our self! Where we meet the underlying stratum, innate tendencies, the natural bedrock of ourselves, we encounter the realities that call into question our limited assumptions. Here we meet the beyond ourselves that enters our lives and moves us. These natural persistencies are fascinating. They border our understanding and, as we shall see, shape our experience, and hence shape our lives.

My findings are drawn from myself and the people I know. Though you and I differ in the details of our images, dreams, fantasies, etc., the underlying processes are the same. How this material is elicited and used is essentially the same for all of us. One of my underlying purposes is to make these regions of the psyche accessible and usable to others. Fairly explicit directions will be given for using your own psyche's abundant clues. Though I am a clinical psychologist, I would like to see mental health experts become less necessary as people find how they can understand themselves. People are generally too impatient and too ready to impose meanings on their psyche to learn from it. And unfortunately, the psyche cannot help but speak a language richer than our understanding. I'd prefer that persons find a modicum of understanding through themselves than a greater wisdom from the purchased friendship of experts.

My special area in psychology is phenomenology. The phenomenologist makes a profound effort to capture, describe, and understand experience just as it is. His work is really protoscientific, coming before science. He raises questions and brings forth material that science can later attempt to bring within objective experimentation. In many respects it is unfortunate that the science of psychology imitated the methods of physics, because it long ago had to abandon looking at the psyche and it doesn't do too well even now with bits of observable behavior. As a humanist and a phenomenologist I feel that living experience is adequately observable. It is so central that I'm willing to forego statistics and the scientific method in favor of understanding experience directly. When the methods of science can reach this domain, then they are welcome. Meanwhile the territory of human experience will have to be mapped by an accuracy less than the surveyor's transit. But, for such a little-known area, hand-drawn maps drawn by venturers on foot will be of much use. If one has an eye for consistency, one can see a remarkable similarity in the ancient maps of religion and the more nearly modern ones of Swedenborg, William James, Sigmund Freud, and modern phenomenologists. Yet, in spite of adequate rough maps, the territory of the psyche is endlessly rediscovered by each individual. No description of human experience should be credited until it checks out with one's own experience. Each person is the final criterion. But phenomenological maps do facilitate one's own discoveries by looking at what merely more patient explorers have found.

The profound inward consistency in the operations of psyche is perhaps a map of maps. The persistent, gentle, ever-present psyche describes our existence at every turn. Why? Because that is its nature, what it is. Human existence is the finding of itself everywhere. But we are getting ahead of the story.

2

The Mystery of Ordinary Experiencing

The external affections of thought manifest themselves in
bodily sensation, and sometimes in the thought of the mind,
but the internal affections of the thought from which the external exist never make themselves manifest to man. Of these he
knows no more than a rider asleep in a carriage does of the
road or than one feels the rotation of the earth. Now, when
man knows nothing of the things beyond number that take
place in the interiors of his mind, and the few external things
which come to the sight of his thought . . . how can anyone
assert that one's own prudence does all things? Were you to
see just one idea laid open, you would see astounding things,
more than tongue can tell.

  Emanuel Swedenborg, *Divine Providence* (¶ 199), 1764

Let's see—I am puzzled what to say. My fingers are clamped
over my mouth and I stare at the things in my study with a hard
feeling of determination. My head feels hot, as it does when I'm
concentrating. What am I to say about ordinary experiencing?
I scan several notes scattered on my desk. Still the fingers
clamped over my mouth and the feelings of hard determina-

tion. Bits of ideas come to consciousness. "Why not start out with—an example of ordinary experience? No. That moves too fast. It sweeps over a number of mysteries as though each was understood." I sit back in my chair and swallow. Now a single finger is clamped over my lips. "I'll have to do both—show the range of things, and then show how each is not fully comprehended."

The whole tenor of this experience was set by the felt need to write. The fingers *clamped* over my mouth was a spontaneous outward representation of my state. The tone of the state was hard, determined. Yet I did not know what to say. The hard gesture reflected the determination (clamped) as well as not knowing what to say (lips covered). Later, when I was more nearly ready to write, there was only one finger guarding the mouth. Staring at the things in the study, searching notes, and scanning ideas that came to me all had the same implications. My response to a felt problem (how to write of ordinary experience) was rapidly and spontaneously represented in a number of ways (hand on mouth, staring, searching notes, checking ideas coming to me, hot head, feeling of hard determination). What I could not see at first later emerged as a conflict in directions—whether to describe the whole flow of experience or to capture one bit of it accurately. The response to the conflict was to move back in my chair (association—sit back and take another look) and swallow (association—try to digest this). The resolving of two trends into one came as I clamped one finger over my mouth. The solution was to accept both trends as part of one.

What I have briefly described was an ordinary experience. The first thing to note is that it represents itself spontaneously and simultaneously on several levels at once—gesture, bodily sensations, inward feeling, actions taken, ideas emerging, self-reflection, and decision-making. This in itself is quite remarkable. We are something that can represent itself in several ways simultaneously. This occurs whether we pay much attention to these ways or not. In fact, we often focus on one ("I wonder what I should say?") and hardly notice the other representations. In other words, though we exist on several levels simultaneously, we may choose to focus on one or more of these as the real, main, or only level.

This limiting of self to a single prominent level is done so commonly that many forget the greater complexity of experience. Because we explain ourselves in verbal terms, the verbal level has become preeminent. In the above instance, if asked "What are you doing?" I would have been inclined to answer "Just working on a problem." The verbal answer is coded shorthand for a complex process all of whose parts are not necessarily even known. The reliance on the verbal as the main or only level of internal processes leads some to think that thought is just unspoken words. Let us focus closer on them.

Phenomenology represents a serious effort to capture human experience just as it is. When the effort of phenomenology is focused on a tiny portion of human experience it acts like a psychological microscope. When I focus the microscope on the formation of words in my head, the bit I would choose is the sudden appearance of ideas. What is it really like when an idea becomes conscious enough that it can be said to myself internally, or externally spoken of?

"I am now formulating this sentence." I felt the general tenor of this sentence before I had finished writing the one before it. It felt like a simple declarative beginning—almost too simple, rather naked and alone. I began to hear it inwardly before it was set down. It was as though I were listening to someone speak. The tenor of the words was felt before they were said, the laying out of meaning was there before they were spoken in my head, and they were said in my head before they were written. These are like successive waves of clarification, each one running over the one before. The whole process took perhaps less than a second. The ending of the sentence also trailed off in a slightly scary feeling. It was as though the gap from the end of one sentence to the next was a little frightening until the next one came.

Focus your own phenomenological microscope on the simple process of thinking up a sentence. See if the process isn't something like the following:

There is a feeling of a need for something.

There is a background feeling it is coming.

The feeling becomes a presentiment of meaning.

The felt meaning germinates into internal speech.

The internal speech lays out a sentence—the end of which is felt while the first part is being heard.

If the sentence is to be spoken, the not-yet-spoken parts are going through stages of being felt, emerging understanding, being heard, spoken.

After the sentence there is a trailing off of feeling, meaning, like an afterglow.

All this may seem like pedantic detailing. Yet it has profound implications. What I would normally think I thought up is really the result of a more complex growth of feelings into words. The feelings are mine, I guess. I have so little idea of their nature, structure, origin, or future directions that it is perhaps presumptuous to say they are mine. It might be more accurate to say I am theirs!

Furthermore, if we sort through the catalog of processes we have cleverly named as existing in people's experience, all of them stem from feeling. Attitudes are a more or less permanent feeling toward things. This feeling-attitude tends to condition response. Action is preceded by feeling. We will see later in the hypnogogic state that feeling can be seen shaping words or images. Fantasy tells the story of feeling. Logical processes are a kind of guardedness and structuring of feeling. Memory is very much based on feeling.

It might help clarify the whole catalog of internal processes if they were seen as points in a continuum of differentiation. The vaguest feeling is the undifferentiated end of the continuum. Specific thoughts, words, memories, images, acts are the multiple outputs of the differentiated end of the continuum. These multiple outputs are related (words in my head are related to words said are related to acts, etc.). Essentially it is the underpinnings, the undifferentiated source of these end-products, that is most elusive to us. We more or less identify with the differentiated end-products. Some identify with these products to the exclusion of their feeling source. As we look closer at processes that primarily represent the life of feeling (fantasy, hypnogogic state, dreams), we have more difficulty identifying with this feeling base as our own making. When the feeling base handily spins off symbolic ideas and images it becomes even more difficult to name it as our own doing. Yet, if it is not fully our own doing, then neither are its products (our thoughts, actions, etc.).

The issue is where one will pin one's personal identity. What can one say "Yea, that is myself!" to? If I say "I make these words," then I must defend control over the whole feeling process underlying them. Yet we will see later that feeling can also speak symbolic ideas that few even understand! It is enough to indicate clearly at this juncture that the I—what I really call me-mine and take responsibility for—is best not limited yet. It is a fundamental issue. This is no minor, simple question. One fundamental answer that emerges from the study of many myths, religions, and one's own experience is: let the personal identity be everything and nothing simultaneously. When one carefully explores the boundaries of personal identity they expand beyond all expectations. The broadening of these boundaries may well be the root of wisdom.

When some feel the necessary humility of leaving open their identity, they feel to have a name, to say I, reflects a lack of wisdom. I can bear a name, and sign checks for convenience, and yet not feel bound by this punctilious boundary of self. The book has a cover and a definite title, and yet may talk of remote worlds. We are such books that we can be circumscribed by titles and yet understood as not circumscribed at all. The title is not the limitation, but the way we conceive of our self is.

A very simple and ordinary example that disturbs the conception of our boundaries is the way we are made up of our ancestors. One can conceive of one's hereditary parents and grandparents almost like curious assigned data or a social security number. Yet a careful examination of personal experience shows individuals to be at least partly shaped by their parents and significant others. The perceived parent, the one experienced and lived with, is introjected and woven into the fabric of one's experience. This is both the perceived parent and the real parent. Insofar as the mother is well perceived, it is more of the real mother that is introjected. The individual is also shaped around what the parents transmitted genetically. Beyond the obvious eye and hair color, and the like, we don't know how much of our psychic experience is involved in this transmission. An individual is also shaped in part by the cultural traditions and even subtle mores of the groups he has lived with. In view of this, it would be more accurate to say that, at least in part, we are the confluence of many others. All those "others" can never be fully catalogued. The confluence of their influences is part of the vast, unknown, undifferentiated background world of the individual. The differentiated individual is the resultant. We are coming under the influence of many others by our increasing participation in the media. How much we are shaped by the cultural matrices we exist in is only now becoming clear with the growth of anthropology and sociology.

However we split it, the boundaries of the self are relatively vast and unclear. But for appropriate convenience we set them at the skin. What is inside the skin is mine, outside it is other.

14

Since I perceive and react to others and am really compounded of others in several ways, this skin boundary should be viewed as a useful fiction. It is the same as saying a book is bound by its covers. This is true enough if one wants to take the most limited view of the book, but it overlooks its contents, where they came from, and the effects they might have on the worlds of others.

The apparently simple issue of what is the boundary of the individual is best left open. Any closing of it is an artificial limiting of our conception. The individual is at the confluence of heredity, parents, significant others, his culture, language, schooling, and the media. He is transcended by these, and in many real respects he is their resultant. When we look closely at the simplest of human experiences we find the so-called individual also transcended within by sensations he doesn't plan and by feelings that seem the general background and source of his experiencing. Consciousness is the running, moment-by-moment bit of clarity and awareness at the confluence of these forces. One's own words emerge out of a sea of feeling—meaning—presentiments. We are the meeting place of at least a number of transcendencies. The discovery of this should not be a matter of great pride or despair. It is just things as they are.

I once worked with a man in a legal experiment on the effects of the drug LSD. We were in a relatively barren hospital room. It took me a while to discover that the man was going around the room quietly naming things. "That is a chair," he would say to himself. Under LSD everything had become too lively and a little frightening. He pinned them down and limited their existence by naming them. He might as well have said, "You are *only* a chiar." I fear our hanging an identity on the sequential confluence of transcendent experiences does about the same thing. Naming implies that we have comprehended, circumscribed, delimited, put down. Naming the chair doesn't mean I really understand how it is made or what it is. It says, in effect, you are of the class of things I've seen before. Of course self or personal identity is also of the class of things I've seen before—whatever it is!

But watch my fingers writing. Theoretically I know how they move. Brain to nerve to muscle, etc. Brilliant. I theoretically understand how I move! Yet secretly I don't really understand brain, nerve, or muscle. Practically speaking, do I know how I move? Well, let's see. I feel the finger pressing the pencil, moving it over the paper. The movements are very fast, but barely able to keep up with inner speech. I pause a moment, resting the hand, watching to see what else will come out of inner speech. I seem to be just this sequence of experiences: feeling, to inner speech, to finger movements. I am this coming together, whatever it is! This confluence seems to be conscious of the meeting. The confluence is experiencing is consciousness. I am the confluence that is consciousness that is experiencing what is here. Yet when this consciousness examines in detail any aspect of its experience it does not fully comprehend or rule it.

Our experience has flowing into it more than we generally understand. It is the same with our body. Though we live in it, move it, and indeed are it, we don't fully understand a single organ of it, nor indeed a single cell. Whatever this experiencing is called man, it is only beginning to open up the nature of its experience because it is transcended at every hand. Though it can name experiencing or consciousness, these too it does not understand.

If you have followed my arguments, you may have several possible reactions.

1. You can't really see that anything transcends you. In which case I would charge you to examine fully a single thought as it emerges. If your thoughts are too fast for you, try to slow them down, and examine several hundred of them. If you get handy at that, then examine examining. Tiring of that, try to hold one thought in mind for five minutes and record all the places your

mind wandered off to and try to see the blanknesses that proceed wandering.

2. You are puzzled that I seem to call into question conventional ideas of the boundary of personal identity. It will not be nearly so difficult or threatening to explore the further operations of mind if the boundaries of self are left open.

3. You feel bothered, or better yet crushed, by the idea that you are transcended at every quarter. One becomes accustomed to this, and, like open boundaries, it removes impediments.

So much for very ordinary experience that represents itself and exists on many levels, in many ways easily and spontaneously—whatever IT is.

3

To See and Hear Another Person

... when, therefore, the thought flows down into the body, it is represented by gestures and actions.... The affections belonging to the mind, are represented in the face, through the various expressions of the countenance.... Internal things are those which are represented, and external things those which represent.

      Emanuel Swedenborg, *Heavenly Doctrine* (¶ 261), 1758

The faces of angels are the forms of their interiors ... an angel who excels in wisdom instantly sees the quality of another from his face.

      Emanuel Swedenborg, *Heaven and Hell* (¶ 47–48), 1758

Perhaps the single most important basic skill that should be taught to all persons is the capacity really to see, hear, and understand others. Such a skill is useful in dealing with everyone—friends, relatives, or strangers. It enables one to understand a person more readily, bypassing much conversation and doubt. It enables one to respond more appropriately to others' needs. A friend may say all is going well with him, but you may see anxiety or depression in his face or gesture. A few gentle words reflecting what you see will deepen and make more real the whole basis of your relationship. What you might otherwise take as a deliberately obstinate attitude in another person may be backed by a consistent bodily rigidity. You can then see the attitude is not just directed against you, but it is part of the individual's whole life. The one seen and heard is generally better off when well understood. Your responses then fit where the other person is rather than where he's supposed to be.

Some may feel that this smacks of an invasion of privacy. Such people are most likely to put too much expertise into the hands of the observer, "They almost have X-ray eyes, they can see your inner thoughts." When we examine the matter we will find several safeguards. The whole business of seeing and hearing others is "guesstimates" and approximations. With considerable practice and skill one can just begin to recognize the mood, feelings, and attitude of the other person. Mind reading, if it exists, is not part of this. These approximations are quite tentative. The good observer is shifting his tentative guessing moment by moment.

But there are deeper and more important safeguards. It is very difficult to divine the mood or attitude of another person without empathizing with it—coming to feel like the other person. This is not a position for dominance or control over others so much as it is one for understanding. In fact, the need to dominate and control others will tend to interfere with the kind of empathy that leads to accurate perception. A common fear of people is that they will be misunderstood. And rather than be misunderstood, they would prefer to be understood only superficially. Real understanding on the part of another person eases and shortens communication, it takes the strain out of it. A person who feels empathetically understood is generally ready to open up and reveal himself at a deeper level. The image of the gimlet-eyed, Svengali mind reader is that he wants to exert some sort of alien, dangerous control over one. The empathetic listener gives the feeling of pleasure of someone trying to understand another's situation. The relationship warms up, the level of concern can deepen; the whole tone of the relationship can get more flexible, playful, or feelingful.

I've taught observation to many mixed groups and my points are illustrated by what I see in people around me. Most are a little fearful at first of what I might see and say about them. They readily learn that my observations are quite tentative and uncertain, which makes them feel better. Most take it up like a fun game and bend special efforts to see friends. They like to comment on my frequent gestures to see how well I know myself. If you are going to observe others closely, it is fair that they will try to do the same to you. In fact, this reciprocal quality is part of the improved communication. In my experience, those who remain uncomfortable at knowing they will really be seen and heard are a unique lot. They fear both understanding and misunderstanding. They have little capacity to look within and fearfully misapprehend their own impulses. They are also afraid of what they might find, and hence are also afraid of what any skilled observer might find. In a world of widespread understanding between persons, they should be permitted to shroud themselves under a total, shapeless cover. Yet by looking at their movement the observer should be able to infer much! Many do hide under the shapeless cover of "I am fine, how are you?" with a pleasing smile. The smile says, "I am not going to hurt you, so don't hurt me."

The ability to see and hear others well is not limited to any one professional or nonprofessional group. It is the stock in trade of psychotherapists. Politicians and diplomats use it. Door-to-door salesmen develop very rapid "diagnostic" skills. It is used by the housewife raising children (or a husband). Any clerk, ticket taker, salesgirl in a store, waitress, and the like who has an opportunity to watch hundreds and thousands of people may develop an acute sense of others' reactions. Old-time yacht salesmen tell me they can tell whether a customer is interested in sail or power boats because their behavior is quite different. I once was very impressed by a professor of veterinary medicine who was teaching a student how to observe a horse. Though the student and I gave the horse our full attention, the professor really could see nuances of the gait missed by both of us.

Contrary to popular opinion, we are presented with too many clues to the nature of other people. We dismiss much of this wealth of information and generally use the most untrustworthy source: what the person says. To compensate for this unfortunate, culturally taught bias, I will emphasize every other way of understanding a person! When I speak of hearing another person, my main emphasis is on how he makes sound, the rhythm and intonation of his voice, not the words. His gestures and voice quality also tell me whether there is any importance in what he says and whether it is probably true!

As a boy in San Francisco, I traveled everywhere on streetcars, which meant many long boring rides. I designed a game that later proved useful. For example, an old lady gets on the streetcar and sits down. Just to pass the time, I become her for a little while. I study everything about her, and reconstruct my world as this old woman.

My tattered cloth shopping bag is precious; it contains food for a week. I put it between my legs to hold onto it. I have to hang on—these cars jerk so—thin hands hanging onto a nearby pole. I look around, trying to see how far we have come, but I can't see well, and gaze again at the week's groceries. The car lurches and I hang on, feeling frail; one slip and I would fall, breaking my bones. So noisy. So confusing. Check the bag, hang on, I'll soon be home. Because I see and hear poorly and am frail, the world is close and small, its lurching clatter a threat. My clothes are very old-style, black hat with beadwork on it, black coat and satin dress, and high button shoes. These are what I am accustomed to. So much noisy confusion. I mustn't miss my stop. Soon I'll be safe at home, behind a locked door. If I can just get off without getting hurt.

Then a burly man in his thirties got on the streetcar. Now, suddenly, I am so big and strong, with so much unused power, that riding the streetcar is like being imprisoned in a tinker toy. With my big chest and arms, I would feel more comfortable breaking cement with a sledge hammer.

In this way I'd try to note every detail of another person and take on his or her characteristics in my mind's eye. Sometimes I would even try the person's movements—try the tremor of an aged hand that has so little power to grasp things.

As an adult, this game was very useful to me in dull administrative meetings. There I played it out in much finer detail. I could spend thirty minutes studying how one person held a cigarette. I would guess, hypothesize, construct, and then find a dramatic moment when the way he flicked off the ash in an ashtray and what he said confirmed my impressions.

Later my task was to train psychiatric nurses in observing patients. We could hear and see an unknown person being interviewed on the other side of a one-way mirror. The nurses at first felt powerless when I turned off the sound and asked them to concentrate their attention on just the movements of a woman's right hand. I forced them to notice every detail and then guess. After great hesitation their guessing gradually zeroed in on the major dimensions of the woman's life. They were pleased and a little surprised to find their impressions confirmed in what the woman said and in her psychiatric history.

There are a number of simple keys to use if you want really to hear and understand another person.

1. Check on your state as an observer. If you have any strong mood, worries, or preoccupations you probably won't observe well. If you must impress others with your skill, you are

likely not to do well. The most productive attitude is one of a relaxed curiosity that notes every detail in the other person.

2. Make every effort to feel into the other's situation. You may immediately feel the other's situation or discover it by subtly trying his or her gestures, imagining that you move and talk like the other, or verbally going over the person's characteristics: "Now I am a stooped ninety-year-old woman, shoes run down at the sides, hard of hearing. . . ." If you accomplish this step, you should lose most awareness of yourself and gain an intense awareness of the other person.

3. Assume every detail is important. It might be enough to see clearly the movement of a single hand or go over and over the intonation of a single sentence. I strongly suspect that the whole nature and quality of a person's life is in every detail of his face, gesture, or voice quality. You might go over any detail that strikes you until you can find no more meaning in it.

4. Guess freely what it would be like to be the other person. A major difference between great and poor empathizers is that the great are more ready to guess.

5. Be ready to shift impressions as new ones come. You are guaranteed to fail if you form an impression and then bend all efforts to get evidence to prove it right.

6. Impressions that seem to be supported in several ways should be held to more firmly than those that get little further support. The reiteration of the same theme from various observations (internal consistency) tends to suggest accuracy.

7. Practice observing friends and relatives first. You should know them well enough to read what is known of them back into gestures and voice quality. One difficulty with friends and relatives is that one tends to dismiss too much, i.e., not

see and hear them! Then practice on strangers, where you will have much less chance to check if you are correct.

8. People vary widely on how together they are. Some exemplify a single drama. Gesture, voice, words, and actions all tend to tell the same story. Some are at odds with themselves. Gesture says one thing and their words another. This discrepancy represents an unconscious conflict. By asking persons which aspect they are most aware of, one can tell what is more or less conscious.

The Face

After words, the facial expression is the feature most often observed. Like words, it is part of our social front, the mask we wear to create the right impression. When we greet a friend, we are supposed to smile. If we really want to impress a friend, then we put on an animated happy face. We are all more or less accustomed to reading the face as part of normal communication.

Individuals vary widely in the use of their faces. Some always have much the same expression. Some allow inner feeling to be fully expressed, almost asking the onlooker to notice pain or sullen hurt. Others allow their faces gradually to become set masks that express little feeling. The amount of play of feeling across the face varies widely. It is very great in the infant and usually declines as one grows toward maturity. The most consistent emotional state tends to become inscribed on the face permanently with age. I can recall older faces that seemed to express chronic disapproval as though nothing in the world were ever quite right. I can also recall an old woman whose joyous, open, happy face seemed to reflect a lifetime of childlike happiness. The most common face is masklike, one in which sober reflection has replaced feeling. It is a poker face, for safely playing the game of life.

It is relatively easy to see the mood or feeling of another person in his face. But one needs to bear in mind that the face is under somewhat conscious control. It may be the mood or feeling the person wants to show. A relatively artificial face in a woman goes with time-consuming make-up and an overinflected "Yes, isn't that wonderful!" kind of expression. Both the make-up and the overplayed feeling suggest that she is working hard to control the responses of others. The seductive expression of a person who seems to have fallen in love with you and yearns for you on first glance also suggests a seductive power play. In contrast, one feels much more secure with the face that seems to represent more naturally the individual's mood and ideas. When saying something serious, the face is serious. When in doubt, the face shows doubt, and so on. The face is allowed to reflect the person clearly.

Much can be learned from the eyes. If there were a circle of people looking at you, you should be able to gauge the psychological distance to them merely from their eyes. In one individual the eyes seem to come forward, to be near you and show trust. In another the eyes are more distant, showing reserve and limited trust. Yet a third person may have vacant eyes directed at you, as though the owner is somewhere else and his eyes are looking at you just to be polite. The felt distance from the others has nothing to do with physical distance. It is really the distance to the real person. The eyes of a stranger may suggest that you could easily cross the room, put a hand on the person's shoulder, and converse. Another closer to you may have eyes suggesting "Keep your distance until I figure you out better." There are very extroverted eyes that seem to reach outward and introverted eyes that seem to see inward as well as outward. The latter reminds you of a person peeping through window blinds from some distance.

One certainly should be able to see strong feeling in the face. It enlivens the face with a tremulous liveliness. Tearful feelings almost instantly redden the eyes and make them look watery. The subject's most common response is to try to close down his face, to hide the intense feeling until it can be brought under control. Fatigue also should be fairly apparent in the faces of others. The face has a sagging, hanging-down quality. To see two contrary feelings in the face is difficult. For instance, a person may put on joyful happiness at seeing you and yet show an underlying depression or fatigue. Both features are present. The joyful expression is put on at the expected time, but the other expression tends to show at less guarded moments. Most valuable also is the discovery in another's face of what really matters. Here the face takes on a very natural and lively intensity. Contrary to the "put-on" face, it may barely be under the individual's control. It may include fleeting tearfulness and efforts at emotional control. The observer is particularly surprised to find this face suddenly in the midst of a random conversation over matters that seemed unimportant. When this occurs to me I zero in on the general area that apparently caused the reaction in an attempt to bring to light the real significance for the individual.

Clothes

Words, face, and clothes are all part of the social front of the individual. Unless you are destitute and have no choice of clothes, they reflect much of how you want to be seen by others. There are a few individuals whose behavior and dress reflect that they don't care a fig for appearance. I recall a distinguished psychiatrist friend of mine who buys suits at rummage sales. He puts on an overcoat when the air gets cold in the late year and it stays on until spring has clearly sprung. He has simplified his life. He wears ties to work, but there is no thought of their possible match with a blue denim work shirt or his two-dollar tweed suit. His friends get used to the fact that he isn't in the clothes game at all. He wears a tie only because his boss thinks a distinguished psychiatrist should pretend to play the game. In contrast there are others whose clothes are some kind of social statement. Young people now favor worn-out jeans with bright patches sewn over gaps. These clothes say something like "I am of the new breed. We are against accumulating wealth, social pretension, and wastefulness." One can fairly well guess their attitudes toward a number of the topics of the day.

There is a great silent majority who wear clothes that reflect what is safe, accepted, common. It is as though they don't want to stand out and be too noticed. They would feel very uncomfortable in faded jeans with a red patch in the seat. At home they wear knockabout casual things, at work a suit and tie or modest dress. They fit in either place, having shifted anonymous styles for each setting. Some show just a trace of wanting to be noticed—a bright tie with the suit, or, in a woman, an unusually attractive hairdo with modest clothes.

The clothes narcissist should be apparent at a glance. In a man, for instance, it could mean big rings, gold wrist watch, meticulous clothes, well-placed tie pin, polished shoes, complete with rather exhibitionistic show-off movements. A heavy emphasis on clothes and appearance is probably less significant in women because they are trained in this direction by society. If a woman has less than usual interest in clothes, it is somewhat unusual and more of a personal statement. The full implication of clothes narcissism is not vain self-assurance. It reflects a concern with what others think of you or a need to create an acceptable image. If this clothes concern is exhibited for others it implies uncertainty, anxiety, and even a hollowness within. The more integrated person chooses clothes (spouse, furniture, house, job, interests) that accurately reflect his own values.

The most interesting clothes reflect the whole style of the person, as though one could see the inside and outside simultaneously. I am reminded of a hippie leader with trimmed beard, beads, and hand-stitched jacket that seemed to present a unique and harmonious image. The clothes really fit the man.

As in other areas of observation, clothes may reflect contrary statements. I've seen many criminal psychopaths with expensive suits that didn't go well with stained ties and wrinkled shirts. The individual didn't have it all together. He wanted to make an impressive appearance, but he was really more of a slob. This is true in a more subtle way with persons who try to play the clothes game but lack taste as to what is really harmonious. More pitiful to see are poor people who try to keep up appearances but can't afford decent clothes. The frayed collar and cuffs of a man and the cracked plastic handbag of a woman in the employment office reflect a more desperate situation.

In women (more clearly than in men) clothes reflect self-esteem. When a woman who characteristically dresses up to the norm lets her clothes go, her spirits may be down. It makes entirely good sense to treat sagging female spirits by a trip to a beauty salon and dress store. Because clothes are chosen by the person they reflect something of choice, the social front, and less of the underlying disposition. This is particularly true of clothes on formal occasions. For a better picture of the underlying disposition, look at a person's clothes on days off, or better yet, his movements, expression, and manner of speech.

Body Movements and Gestures

An individual's physical body is his fundamental given. I look to see what is given and how it is used. In the male I look at the hands, arms, shoulders, neck, abdomen, and legs to get an overall impression of basic physical power. Even without seeing a man undressed, it is relatively easy to determine if he is physically strong, has muscles and flab, or is mostly flab. Inferences as to his life-style can be made immediately. The curve of the neck into the shoulders, though mostly concealed beneath clothes, could imply massive physical strength. If the body is thin or small I would look at the bones and ask myself if he was potentially big but undernourished or was his given physique small? Next I would watch gestures to see how he used his body. One man enjoys physical strength and uses it easily. Another has effeminate gestures as though he would wish to be built differently. The small man may overcompensate by making big gestures, making his presence felt. If there is a physical disablity, I'm interested in learning what the disability means to the person. One may be blind and live as though sighted; another would consider a minor blemish to be a lifelong tragedy.

Corresponding to the musculature of men I look at the rounded curviness of women. A heavy, full, matronly figure may suggest matronly behavior until one looks closer at accompanying gestures. Women with a thin layer of fat, thin skin, and apparent muscles tend to be athletic in one way or another. I have long speculated on the importance of the size of a woman's bosom. Whatever it relates to in personality, it doesn't seem to have much to do with motherliness! Some women seem heavy below the waist in comparison with the upper part. These women seem more earthy, earthbound. The implications of the body set the beginnings of speculation on the lives of others. In Europe the science of reading personality from aspects of the body is called physiognomic psychology. It is little known and little believed in the United States.

Gesture is complex and revealing, and I will not be able to go into all its implications here. The usual pace of the gestures is related to the pace at which one lives. If I had to choose laborers to do much work and had only one criterion, I would want to see them walk across the room. One of the most unproductive people I know had a slow drawl in his movements. It looked as though his legs would saunter along in infinite leisure and the upper part of the body hung back from even this pace! Those who have waited for waitresses know that some almost cannot move fast. Others can barely move slowly.

Characteristics of a person's walk are often neglected, but most can recognize the sound of a relative's walk. Some beat the ground with their feet. Some very cerebral people seem barely to touch ground. Some are always of the same timing or pace. Others vary widely, as they do in their inner life. Those who are always in the future, thinking about what must be done, planning, working toward future goals, tend to bend forward when walking, as though the upper part is ahead of the lower. A woman I knew who was given to frequent illegitimate pregnancies swung her pelvis in an interesting way and led with it.

Hands are very interesting to watch as a person speaks. They may come forward and cleverly elaborate a point. They may show tension or be thrust forward as though attacking. A little gesture like the hand over the mouth has many possible meanings. It may say "I'm thinking," or "I'm unsure what to say," or "I'd better be careful what I say." The hand playing in and around the mouth may just be part of the person touching, feeling himself, or fingers in the mouth may be a kind of self-nurturing act. It would be convenient if a gesture always meant one thing. But gestures differ as much as people. A gesture that is often seen as defensive is arms crossed on the chest. It can mean a walling in, protecting, or awkwardness of hands and arms solved by tying them up, simply conserving body warmth, etc. The meaning of a gesture is clearer in the whole context of a person's behavior; dictionary interpretation of one gesture meaning one thing is foolish.

The vigor and mood of a person is relatively easily seen. If a person were dissembling—feeling depressed but acting convivial—one should be able to see the downward mood covered by a veneer of vigor and interest. In this case the movements may taper off and droop too soon, lacking a sustained vigor. Or movements can be too brisk, outgoing, verging on the uncontrolled. A man with such movements once wanted to borrow money from me. I figured I wouldn't get it back.

I've done formal examinations of many people who wanted to impress me. Behind the façade of a routine conversation, they weren't aware that I was watching them put ashes in an ashtray. See this intensely reflective man, putting out a butt slowly, carefully pressing down on the end. Another was an obsessive-compulsive man, putting the cigarette out, checking if it is out, putting it out again, and then cleaning up scattered ashes. The details of the act caught and trapped him. He couldn't feel quite satisfied it was done right. Here was an alcoholic with a criminal record. While acting with deference and politeness he was dropping cigarettes on my floor, and scattering ashes. His gestures said he was really inconsiderate.

Take just smoking alone. There is a considerable difference between the one who has a desperate quality about getting the cigarette in his mouth and the one who is tripping off in fantasy behind the smoke. Some take in the smoke meditatively. Others are in an impatient, irritable battle between themselves and the cigarette, which is grabbed, stuffed in, hastily puffed on, and smoke blown out. I used to observe my boss; just where in the conversation he would make a desperate-looking grab for his cigarettes in his left coat pocket. The gesture came when he felt tired, spent; he wanted to be finished with the matter at hand and tend his own needs. It was a good time to end the conversation and leave. The thinkers I enjoy dealing with carefully, slowly, break off the ash and study its softness and its form. Then I know I'm meeting their greatest thoughts, slowly and carefully developed, feeling out every nuance. I would guess those with a kind of intense relationship to a cigarette—it is grabbed, stuffed in, used up with little awareness—have the most difficulty in stopping smoking; for it satisfies unconscious needs for them.

There is a great deal about the body that is not well known. One example are the taboos around body zones. We all know where we can touch a friend or a stranger. On a man we can touch most of his arm (armpits a little forbidden), shoulders, neck, and upper torso. In a woman the permissible areas are more restricted. Two zones around the breast are restricted to lovers, physicians, and infants. The boundary of these areas is quite definable. A man can touch a woman progressively toward the breast, and both the man and woman can specify when the forbidden boundary line is reached, agreeing within a half an inch or an inch.

When the don't-touch zones are drawn on the body, a funny picture emerges. In the face, the eyes, inside the nose, mouth, and ears are forbidden unless okayed by the person who owns the face. In the female the breast area and the tissues immediately leading to it are forbidden. The genital area is taboo in both sexes as are the anal region and buttocks. The lower leg has no taboos except perhaps between the toes. The upper leg is taboo only insofar as one is approaching the genital area and buttocks. In other words, all the body openings, and anything to do with sex, are taboo. Creases or folds in the skin (between toes, fingers, under arms) are slightly taboo. All this is consistently conveyed from generation to generation without much or anything being said of it. All the broad, relatively flat expanses of the body are not taboo. Taboos begin around implied openings (between the toes) and get quite clear around real openings. Areas of the body that have little opening (i.e., the male's penis) but have strong sensory feeling are chief among the taboos. It is as though the body were a castle and all the doors and windows were guarded by custom.

Very little is known about the language of the body in space. For instance, if everyone in the room were asked to tilt his head to the left and interiorize the feelings and attitude represented by this position, most would come out with similar meanings. "To the left I feel tolerant, patiently sizing up something I didn't understand. I'll allow the other person the benefit of the doubt." Head tilted to the right has a related but opposite meaning. "I don't quite believe you. What you say surprises and shocks me. I have trouble accepting it." A host of meanings surround standing up and how one occupies and uses space.[1] To stand straight upright implies one is ready and in command of this space. Any other kind of bending, lounging, etc. implies one is using the space, but not in full command. Schizophrenics who are locked up within a head full of fantasy and hallucinations have trouble getting down to and comfortably using the ground as a base of support. Some of these meanings show in projective tests. For instance, when asked to draw a human figure on a blank page, the unusual addition of a ground line under the feet shows that the individual is unsure of his bearings and support within the world.[2] When asked to draw designs on paper, the paranoid who has trouble disentangling himself from others may draw in rare boundaries between the designs.[3]

To my knowledge only the European phenomenologists have thrown much light on this murky area of the silent meanings of man in space.[4] For the most part this is a relatively undiscovered area. One great importance of this area is that a disorder in one's relationship to the world can be discovered in the body as shown in bioenergetic psychotherapy.[5] Moreover, a direct shift in how one uses the body tends also to shift the inner attitudes and experiences! This same knowledge is also contained in ancient systems such as yoga and T'ai Chi Ch'uan.[6] In T'ai Chi one learns and practices a long series of graceful dancelike movements that depict one in mock combat with the world. One learns a graceful way of coping with the world. We are so wont to think of ourselves as making the body do as we will that it is a shocking comedown to discover that the body also makes us do its will.

The given body probably relates to one's given potential. Gesture and movement are the much more expressive and subtle indications of how the potential is being used. Rather than making gesture do as we wish, much of it expresses less conscious habit.

Voice Quality

The voice quality of an individual is one of the most neglected, least understood, and more effective ways of understanding an individual. Voice quality refers to all aspects of speech but the word content. It includes rhythm, intonation, areas of emphasis, and all the subtle nuances that make an individual's voice unique. Those who observe voice quality may use the voice quality to check on the probable validity of what was said. There is not much literature in this field and voice quality is difficult to describe in print. A recording giving examples of different voices would be more effective.

Because it is not generally known that voice reflects personality, there is relatively little conscious manipulation of the voice. Most of it is found in those who train their voice for public presentation. The older style was to develop an overinflected voice, one that would make minor matters sound like life-and-death matters. Some of the older newscasters have this quality. Some ministers develop a pulpit voice that is also overinflected. It has the quality of a poor actor who displays more feeling than he actually feels. Some individuals show the same tendency on a lesser scale. This often goes with exaggerated gestures and excessive eye movements. The simple implication is that the individual wants to make a dramatic impression. The voice lacks the naturally excited quality, say, of children at play. The child feels excited and caught up, and his voice reflects it.

There is a whole range of voices that reflect various relationships to words and meaning. For instance, a person who reflects deeply on what he is saying tends to be slow and measured in his speaking. The opposite would be the flighty thinker who races through bunches of words without stopping or thinking of what he is doing. Most people carefully measure their words at some times. Those who do it all the time enjoy the process of searching out meanings. There are also people who speak as though words were tasty delicious morsels. They tend to enjoy words in themselves. Poetry, drama, or literature impress them. Lawyers and lawyerlike people often enjoy clarifying the logical structure in ideas. They enjoy the laying out and mapping of relationships. In distinct contrast is the muffled, slurred speech of the person who would have difficulty understanding what rationality meant. The pace of the individual's speech is another reflection of his over-all pace. This can vary from halting speech to bursts of words like a machine gun firing.

There is a clear interpersonal side to speech. The person who projects his words, sends them out like darts, is really trying to reach others. In contrast is the more introverted person whose voice quality sounds enclosed, as if he were talking from inside a barrel. Some introverted speakers really sound as though they are talking to themselves. Their voices have a flat, monologic, held-inside-the-mouth quality. They may be hoping that someone happens to overhear their monologue. I don't judge as sick or schizoid the person whose glance is everywhere but toward me, whose manner and voice is withdrawn. His voice says only, "At this moment I am sending a message indirectly to you while I stay at some distance."

There is a great deal more in voice quality that may slowly be discovered. I seem to notice the same thing in the voice that I notice in all the rest of persons. Each detail of the voice, the dramatic way in which a single word is said, seems to be an image of the whole. In the same way gesture could be limited to the movement of one hand and yet recover the main drift of the personality. Just as one could photograph in one's mind's eye a bit of gesture and go over and over it, so one can record the drama of a single word or sentence. When carefully laid out in time, under the phenomenological microscope, the word or sentence contains a whole drama. For instance, a single word has several turns of mood or tempo. In women for whom feeling is the real basis of their life, each word can have distinct emotional turns ending on a lilting upswing. A single word may sound very musical, like a happy song was being sung. In a depressed person each word has a somber turn to it. It might well be enough to hear all the implications in a single word.

To See and Hear Feeling

Since feeling is the key to the inner life and to what is significant to an individual, it is important to underline its role in observation. To deepen a conversation or relationship, concentrate on finding feeling in the other person. Having found it, a simple comment on its presence expands the relationship. For instance, my wife was asking me whether I wanted this or that for dinner. Her gesture suggested that it was not a routine question. She needed to be useful and supportive. A response with that in mind was important to her. A more dramatic example occurred when a young woman asked a question about asthma. I asked if she was bothered by it. As she spoke I noticed many small blockings occuring in the midst of apparently innocent words. With a little effort she could uncover what was being held back as she spoke. We ended with a very tearful release of feeling about the way she feels blocked in many spheres.

Feeling shows in a number of related ways. The face shows a more dramatic emotional quality. The voice may quiver as though feeling were breaking in on the formation of words. Gestures are enlivened and the eye may quickly redden and look tearful. I have interviewed persons with many others looking on. Even though they were looking closely, only a fraction of the onlookers could see feeling. Feeling comes rapidly and shows itself by just faint traces. On the first inquiry the subject may express no awareness of it. The subject felt something, but it was easily dismissed as unimportant. Sometimes this will occur a second time before the subject begins clearly and consciously to experience massive feelings.

A number of things occur in such an apparently simple process. For one, I always reserve judgment until the subject can acknowledge feeling. I may think it is there, but it isn't really there until it shows and the subject acknowledges it. Second, onlookers to such a process tend to be embarrassed and very unsure of themselves when feelings get more apparent. It is as though we have a tacit contract not to arouse each other's feelings. Onlookers will often sense feeling in a subject and then help the subject keep the lid on by changing the subject and getting into some extraneous debate. When strong feeling is released in a subject, onlookers are really caught flatfooted. What can one do to control this process or help the person? This involves a fundamental misunderstanding of what strong feeling is. The person who becomes tearful and cries is in the presence of what matters most to him. If the meaning is not clear to him, I am inclined to say something like, "Please don't try to control the tears. I don't mind your crying. Let us try to understand what is so important in this for you." Tears are meaning bubbling to the surface. They will be beneath the surface as long as meaning is blocked in the individual. When released, there is no need to fear they will flood the world and go on forever. They are a valuable opportunity to discover what is really important to the individual. One doesn't even need to worry about what to do with this meaning. It is the subject's own. Having found what is significant to him, he is in a far better position to decide what to do about it. Some onlookers feel it is cruel to awaken such feeling. Their own cruelty at leaving life buried is far greater. The subject who has experienced a release of feeling-meaning usually feels better after it, and his friends understand him better. Of course this is not something one would do at a casual cocktail party. Should emotional issues arise there, it would be better to note their existence and arrange a private get-together to deal with them.

Anxiety is also visible. In addition to the other signs of increased feeling there is a change in breathing: its depth is restrained. The heavier beat of the heart may be visible in the chest. Again, the individual's tendency may be to try to hold back the disorderly feelings of anxiety. I may ask, "Did you become a bit anxious? You seem to be holding your breath." If the answer is yes then I am inclined to ask if the individual knows what the anxiety was about. One may need to inquire several times before the person becomes aware of his anxiety.

In an ideal society everyone would be able to see feeling and aid feeling-meaning to come forth. Only an emotionally impaired society would leave this to hired experts. It should be everyone's province. When you ask an auto mechanic a series of worrisome questions about your car, a genius Zen mechanic may make you aware of your fears, thereby taking the bulk of the disorder out of the car and finding it in the owner. Having disentangled it from the car, the disorder becomes one's own, within, where it is easier to fix. When one sees a waitress sending out all kinds of signals of distress, it helps to say, "You look impossibly busy—may I have a so-and-so—?" One can see what interests a new acquaintance: it is the subject around which he suddenly shows a greater emotional investment and animation. To see, elicit, and follow the thread of feeling in another person is a key to understanding.

The Amount of Self-awareness

It is not too difficult to gauge roughly the degree of an individual's self-awareness. An individual who is aware of himself senses and monitors the processes occurring within him. This probably goes along with a capacity for awareness of others. Without self-awareness the individual has a simpler, flat, unidimensional picture of himself. The key to gauging the amount of awareness is in what he says of himself in relation to what another can see and hear. For instance, a friend of mine always ground his teeth when speaking of his son. When I mentioned the teeth grinding he was totally unaware of it. He also denied any angry feelings toward his son. He further overlooked that his son was seeing a play therapist because of behavioral problems. He showed no awareness in this area. On another occasion I saw a psychologist who had a most unusual way of making a point in a speech and then holding his mouth open and turning his head slowly from side to side. The gesture looked like a very dramatic underlining of what was important to him. When reminded of the gesture he responded that he had a theory that with his mouth open he would get more air and his head would hurt less. Just jokingly I asked if he could imitate what I had seen. He did a poor job with his mouth barely open. In the original gesture he barely breathed, in contrast to his theory of himself. He had partial insight into his own behavior, and didn't really account for it by a theory. The person with considerable self-awareness, on the other hand, can describe himself just as others see him, including his nuances of gesture and behavior. In fact, having been reminded of a gesture, he can describe much of its background feeling.

Self-awareness is insight. Such persons with little of it are repressed and not insightful. They are more difficult to deal with as persons. Though the onlooker may be able to see and hear much of the nature of their life, he also has to bear in mind his own limited awareness. Persons with greater insight are easier to deal with in depth. They have rich moment-to-moment impressions. There is no defensive hiding. They are available to themselves and to others.

The diagnostic implications of limited insight are not at all clear. I've known psychotic individuals who were nearly knee-deep in insight. But their insights were richly disorganized and not of great use to anyone else. Other psychotics seem to have a most limited and inadequate view of themselves, as though they learned of themselves out of some stilted copybook. Some people are capable of sensitive insight into themselves but prefer not to deal with it. The mentally retarded seem also to range from no self-awareness to a very sensitive responsiveness. Yet, like children, they may find it difficult to portray themselves adequately in words. Anyone who has played with children as a kind of diagnostic study of their world will know that they are very capable of living out and expressing their situation in behavior, but, like the retarded, may be able to present only a simple picture of themselves verbally.

Those with little self-awareness are wont to suspect that self-awareness is something like a plague one should best avoid. In general, self-awareness deepens both the negative and positive sides of one's experience. With it one experiences more, more intensely. While it provides keys to ordinary problems, it also deepens the issues one faces. Aware people see themselves as others see them. If you are curious, they can comment on their voice quality or gesture in ways that enrich your understanding of them. They are aware of nuances of feeling. They have a value system, goals, hopes, fears, all of which they can show you. This is not a matter of intelligence. Some brilliantly intelligent people show little self-awareness; some relatively ignorant and simple people can show amazing insight. One cannot help but respect a person of any station in life who knows himself well. They stand far taller than persons who keep to a narrow copybook picture of themselves.

The Interpersonal Side of Observation

Careful observation of others should not be a one-way street. Usually a person who finds he is understood becomes more animated and more ready to relate to the observer. Often there is a surprised reaction when the subject finds he is being apprehended on a deeper level than usual. Occasionally a defensive person will back away from the relationship. For him the game was to be superficial and any other kind of response is threatening. The observer can handle this sometimes by humor, for it permits communication on two levels at once. For instance, comments reflecting a woman's dark mood caused her to tighten up and back away. The speaker might then respond with, "Now that everyone is feeling happy, we can go on with planning the outing tomorrow." A knowing glance settles the matter. It acknowledges that her mood is down, and that it is not to be talked about.

Sometimes a person who feels unusually well understood will begin to feel that he himself has not been observant enough. So as not to get all the attention, he will switch the conversation to questions of the observer's life. Just as the observer wanted to find the other open, he is in turn obliged to be open himself. If I have learned something quite intimate of another's life, I am ready to share something equally intimate of mine if the other person is interested. Where the other person finds it difficult to be open, one may lead the way by first being open about one's self.

I've had an unusual opportunity to observe professional con men and liars. By now I should have brilliant observations about them, but I haven't. One main clue I've found is the way they respond to our relationship. If I suspect I am dealing with a con man (criminal, salesman), I deliberately vary my manifest mood and even the topic of conversation and observe how well the other person follows. If he can sense and react almost instantaneously to my mood, however subtly it shows, he is overalert to how he is affecting me. If I can switch topics of conversation and he is equally fascinated with whatever I say, then he is really out to manipulate me. The normal person is slow to respond to shifts of mood. Shifts of conversation throw him off. The con man draws you out, and, like a pink mirror, reflects back a pretty image of you. He is tense and alert, constantly measuring how well he's doing. The normal person has his own feelings, interests, and outlook. He tends to stay on his own track. The normal person is not that concerned with what another thinks. He shows some anxiety, some moods, some central concerns. He does not happen to say what you wanted to hear. He is his own person, not one calculated to impress another.

The pleasantest of all contacts are those that acquire some depth. One feels more human in them, and feels that the other is a real person.

The Integration of Observations

Although observations are presented piecemeal, they actually come all at once from a number of aspects of the person. An example might clarify the process.

I met a total stranger at a wedding reception. As we engaged in a light conversation about the bride and groom I noticed a number of things. He was in a suit and tie like every other male, but his pants drooped a bit and his tie was askew. He gave the impression that he was not comfortable in these clothes. He would have liked to dress more casually. His hair was speckled with gray. He must have been about forty-five. His heavy round face was tanned, and his ears and his hands were also tanned. He did something out of doors. There was a heavy solemnness in his manner. As he spoke I got the impression his lips closed easily. He would have preferred not to chitchat. The words and phrases went down at the end. He was six feet tall with a heavy build. More and more I got the impression of an unpretentious outdoorsman, now caught in a situation not to his liking. I asked him what he did. He worked in designing community drug programs. This was presented in a rapid monologue with little animation or voice inflection. I began to guess that he didn't really enjoy his work. Then I heard a slight sigh as he hurriedly dusted off his work. His vocabulary implied education and intelligence, yet his manner was heavy and uncomfortable. I was looking for the explanation of his discomfort. Again, noticing his tan, I said, "Your tan suggests you must do something outdoors." He seemed a little surprised, smiled, moved back, opened out his arms. I knew I was close to what was more meaningful to him. He said that he enjoyed yachting when he had a chance. He eyed me and his breathing was restrained as though he were watching for my reaction. I ask just two more questions about yachting and he became fully animated and comfortable. Though he was a fairly bright and well-known social scientist, he felt trapped in his job. He had a small boat, but he hoped to build a large one in a few years and sail around the world. The world of parties, suit and tie, making an impression, pretension no longer interested him. He was a brilliant peasant who wanted to build a boat and grapple with the ocean. Finally I felt I had met him and understood him. It was difficult for us to part to talk with the other guests. I too felt more simply human.

4

Self-Reflection—Existence Gains from Itself[*]

A thing may be present to a man a hundred times, but if he persistently fails to notice it, it cannot be said to enter into his experience. We are all seeing flies, moths and beetles by the thousand, but to whom, save an entomologist, do they say anything distinct?

William James, *Psychology*

Thought is nothing but internal sight.

Emanuel Swedenborg

The meditation of my heart shall be understanding.

Psalm 49:3

It must be dreadful to be the aware, conscious, wise center of a person and watch that person caught in the grip of circumstances. Most of one's life seems to be the living out of responses to the mean, limited circumstances surrounding one. Whether

*Modified from a chapter in *Experiences in Being*, edited by Bernice Marshall. Copyright © 1971 by Wadsworth Publishing Co., Inc., Belmont, Calif. 94002. Reprinted by permission of the publisher, Brooks/Cole Publishing Co.

in prison, or imprisoned in a job, or in the response to one's limited setting—it is much the same. It is possible to transcend all this and gain from it. It is so easy and so valuable that the art of it has nearly been lost. Self-reflection is a gazing at one's life and circumstances as though it were a painting to be examined, felt, appreciated. In self-reflection the third or inner eye is opened, and one gazes at one's life to learn, appraise, decide.

The habit of self-reflection builds a sanctuary above the street-stores-people–world. One can choose how elaborate and protected a sanctuary it is by the way the habit is cultivated: whether it will be close to the streets, of varying distance from the world, or so grand as to look down on all the worlds.

Self-reflection is a lost art that is hardly considered in all the literature of psychology. It is, first of all, fun. It is very like an animal about to snuggle down in a warm bed. The animal turns, sniffs, and leisurely assesses the qualities of his chosen bed. Self-reflection assesses the bed one is in, the place, the circumstances of one's life. Like the animal, it should be an unhurried, mildly pleasurable snuggling down into the bed, the sanctuary, the way of life one chooses.

Years ago, after a difficult day, I went for an evening walk. The streets were empty, darkness and shadows softened all forms, a cricket's chirp seemed friendly. I could listen leisurely to my footsteps and feel the quiet night air. I thought to myself, what a contrast between the day's stresses and the peace of the evening. It struck me like a brilliant idea that I was free to come back every evening. No matter how bad things got, I could go for a walk and appreciate the subtle forms of evening. I was free to come back to this sanctuary from which I could view the stresses of the world or enjoy the respite of a new and more pleasant world. On other occasions I've looked at rusted machinery for an hour and come away with a feeling for rust and iron and intricate parts ready to mesh with and work with each other. As a man in a strange city I sat on a granite monument and watched people go by for hours in peaceful wonder at the endless variety of human differences. When back in the grip of circumstances, the sanctuary of self-reflection seems evanescent, thin, almost a foolish waste of time. Within the mesh of circumstances self-reflection seems like a pleasant escape perhaps, but of no real use in getting things done. But within self-reflection the grip of circumstances seems unnecessarily tight, limiting, and blinding. From the sanctuary of self-reflection the world's stresses seem like an overplayed drama, another cowboy shootout on Main Street. The relativity of our "worlds" is an issue that will arise again and again.

Under the term "introspection," self-reflection was long ago dismissed by scientific psychology as too unreliable to be worth investigating. When called "contemplation" or "meditation" it has played a major role in most religions. In the Oriental religions meditation was developed into a fine and complex art to obtain unusual states of awareness, as in yoga and Zen. In its most rational, logical, thought-laden form it has issued forth as philosophy. In a real way, all this elaboration and refinement has made self-reflection seem remote and not easily available to the average person. It is described here in its simplest, most basic, and immediately useful form. What is described is already known and used by everyone. In talking about it, though, I give life and stature to what otherwise could seem complex, remote, only for the brilliant. I suspect the mind is like a shallow puddle. Left undisturbed, it quite easily reflects back its surroundings. The trick, if there is any, is to leave it undisturbed. How is it done?

Peaceful leisure is the primary ingredient. The second is to experience what is. And the third is to mull it over.

Like most people, having little peaceful leisure, I've practiced self-reflection in bed at night, while taking a shower, and even while driving down the highway. While driving I fix my gaze on the highway so I can respond to traffic and then inwardly shift into leisure gear. On a particularly long, boring drive I felt depressed and lonely. I allowed my discomfort to elaborate into a fantasy. I became aware of a thin woman in black driving alongside me. As the story deepened I found she was ill, thin from having been forced to do things against her will. I became acquainted with her and comforted her. She gradually cheered up and looked less mournful. Pulling myself away from our fantasy relationship, I realized, of course, that she was my inner self—as real as the inside me. I didn't like the long drive and the task I had at the end of it. Hence my mournful companion was thin, in black, sick at having to do so much against her will. This was the first time I found self-reflection was possible when driving. But it doesn't work as well in heavy traffic! This also illustrates the simple ingredients: leisure, experiencing what is, and then mulling it over.

One may find self-reflection easiest in the morning or evening, whenever leisure is possible. Usually there is an inner calling, a concern, a problem, a question, or just a vague feeling that beckons one. It is as though one feels called upon to look, to feel, to assess. If this is done leisurely, almost without plan or compulsion, in response to an inner feeling, the results are the richest. It's the very opposite of doing a job because it has to be done. It should be like play, like a toddler slowly exploring pots and pans for the first time. The pots and pans of later life are whatever interesting concerns are at hand to be explored.

The most critical question is what to reflect upon. One could grab anxiously at what one felt ought to be examined. The most productive self-reflection works on whatever is uppermost in one's mind. This needs some explaining. One evening I was fresh from a fight with a superior at work. It was difficult to think of anything else. I felt like examining all sides of this situation. This was uppermost. On a number of evenings I survey my opinions and decide what my values are. Sometimes I'll have a dream or a vague feeling that I'll go over. The focus may be simply, "What on earth do I feel now?" The uppermost concern is like the top piece of business on the pile, what one can focus on and stay with for a while. It wants doing. Usually after fifteen minutes of pondering and writing, the concern resolves itself and graduates to a deeper understanding. One implication of this pattern is that the concern in the forefront can be of any nature from a vague feeling to a deep, philosophical question, such as "Is there a God?" It need not even make sense. I can conceive of a person who, feeling like writing nonsense, seriously sits down, writes nonsense, and then considers its implications for him. There should be no preset limits to the subject matter of self-reflection. Anything is game as long as it reflects the fabric of one's existence. In my self-reflections there is absolutely nothing I might not consider: aches and pains, sex, death, God, my faults, my greatness, ghosts, the unreal. The following is an example of when I attack the nature of thought itself.

Let's see, how do thoughts form? I hear them spoken, a word at a time, with a general feeling for the whole sentence before it is completed. Swiftly. There. That's it. Coming forth out of a sea of presentiments. The words, and the information they convey, are like a spotlight picking out details while playing over an amorphous dark background. It isn't as though I operate the spotlight. Rather I am at the words. I am the shifting bit of clarity. I experience the moving clarity, not seeing the light but the images it brings. I dare not think how it all works. It might shut off and I would fall into the sea of presentiments. I feel the sea, but I am not accustomed to questioning it, or the light. There I am alive and dreadfully dependent in the fleeting clarity of bits and pieces. Do I make thought? Perhaps only when I question it, like stirring the sea with my hand, to see its response.

There is a deeper aspect to this kind of self-reflection. It should combine the highest and lowest powers of mind. When I used the analogy of a sanctuary above the streets, I was implying the highest aspect of mind. At this level, mind permits itself to reflect back itself that it might see and judge of itself. This is another dimension of existence in which the person can consider and even reconsider his existence and judge it, even alter his choices. At this level, mind or one's existence becomes aware of and chooses itself. A life without self-reflection is like the blind beating of waves on the shore. But waves that consider their existence can understand sea and land. Without self-reflection one just exists. With it existence awakens, watches, studies, and learns.

When people find that their minds can spin off fantasies, images, or ideas endlessly, they may be impressed by this process alone. But by itself this process means little. Madmen sitting in the back ward of a hospital can spin off more than my mightiest efforts. It is at the point that the mind reflects back, questions, examines, and, yea, judges its own work that the real value is extracted. This is where madmen fail. They cannot stop the spinning off and make any use of it. I could have fantasized a relationship with a somber lady in my car for hours. Certainly an inner feeling was being lived out, but it would have been lived out whether I noticed it or not. The fantasy acquired the greatest use when I saw she represented my inner disposition and accepted it as real. Then I could consider how I might act to make "her" less mournful. Actually her appearance and health improved when I recognized her as me and tried to comfort her. Self-reflection, reflecting back on itself, tries to make as much use as possible out of itself. One can even reflect back on the process of making use, judging, valuing, and judge judging. Everything is fair game.

The quality of richness in self-reflection has two elements:

1. The amount of one's life involved in the material worked on.

2. How much value one extracts from it for one's self. The madman is remarkably strong on point 1, but remarkably weak on 2. Some good but rather dull, useless philosophy comes from

those who work on trivial material (having little of life in it) but extract for a fare-thee-well.

The amount of life in the material reflected on relates closely to how much of the so-called lower aspects of mind are in it. At its best self-reflection, the highest aspect of mind, takes account of its lower aspects, its own foundation. By low aspects I am referring to a host of vague subjective phenomena, feelings, anxiety, dreams, fantasies, weird notions. These are more primitive in that they are half-formed, strange upwellings that may not make any sense to consciousness. The highest function of self-reflection should also take account of, begin with, explore, and eventually judge the lowest aspect of mind. This kind of self-reflection is very different from the published works on philosophy in which a brilliant mind remains on the level of thinking or rationalizing. The following is an example of self-reflection that begins at this primitive level.

In the midst or reading, an image came to mind. Though I was reading of earthquakes at sea, the image was entirely unrelated. I saw a scene in a medieval drama: a terrace outside a mansion, a French courtier —it had the feeling of a small French town. Another recurrent scene, came to mind. I saw a courtyard near a factory at the beginning of the Industrial Revolution. Everything was shut down, quiet. It was empty, sunny, giving a feeling of great peace and leisure. The theme in both scenes was leisure, pleasure, which was what I was doing. I was at sea in my bunk, warm under a wool blanket. Nothing to do. Savor, enjoy. Because I chose to enjoy leisure, pleasure, I visualized scenes of the same nature. They bubbled to the surface to reflect my inner state. The state itself was relatively rare for me—hence perhaps the images were back in time, out of my normal ken.

If you want to become a great contemplative, there are only two other ingredients to add:

1. Do it regularly.
2. Set it down in writing afterward.

Doing it regularly means simply that you will do it more. Setting it down gives it life and substantiality. Or you can be a less great casual contemplative and not write out these reflections, allowing the wonders that issue forth from your mind to blow away like smoke.

It was many years before I came to the idea of writing down these bits of self-reflection. When I thought of it, I discovered that most of the best ideas that bobbed to the surface of my mind sank again and were lost in minutes. I found a good notebook and started noting my ideas. It was as though a whole process that was casual and not too important took on importance. What was a temporary, soon-lost process became permanent. The very reality of vague feelings and half-felt truths that rose near consciousness and strengthened and affirmed. My journal was the place I met myself and took myself seriously. The idea of a written journal came from Gabriel Marcel.[1]

I could see this great French philosopher was simply, persistently trying to understand one idea at a time by painstakingly searching himself. For instance, he did a volume on the mystery of being a person by studying his own personhood. He had to look at his own life in order to open gradually all the unknowns in this experience. There are whole areas of human experience that have never been explored. Feeling especially acquires reality when set down. Perhaps the journal only comes later, when one realizes that one's own reflections are worth something to one's self.

Clearly the journal should not be written for anyone else. That would constrict it. My journal is an encounter with myself. It need not be well written. It need not even make sense to others. It is free ground, ground on which I can wrestle with and consider myself, or my feelings of the world, or analyze feeling itself, or take apart my mind, or consider my toenails, if I choose to. It is not for others. If, like Gabriel Marcel's *Journal* it is of use to others, fine.[2] If not, that is fine too.

If nothing else, I see the style of the journal as removing all the restrictions on writing. "Ja mah mah a ka bla bla." I can say anything I please. In part I find that this very free self-expression aids writing. I believe that this open expression, unlimbering the mind, freeing tongue and pen, can aid one to become a creative writer. But though this may be one result, it is not the main aim.

My real aim is to understand everything. Though I am small and not too wise—and no one believes I can do it—for a few cents I can get pen and paper and attempt it. In the end only I will judge its use. It is a most serious and grand enterprise. Yet it takes only pen, paper, and maybe ten to fifteen minutes every other day or maybe every day. Since you will be boss of your enterprise, do it as you wish. I can only suggest from my experience. I've done best by writing a bit every day. I may be bored or tired and then sit down and study the inside of boredom or tiredness itself. The encounter with myself is friendly, pleasant, sometimes a little frightening. It clarifies where I am and where I am going. Self-reflection should have some heroic quality, like a giant testing his own strength. It should venture into areas of thought and feeling seldom visited by others. It should attack the very basis of existence. It is a secretly great enterprise.

Self-reflection is likely to revolve around several major areas, though this is so free an enterprise that any area could be devised. A key area is the study of feelings, anxieties, dreams, fantasies, or any subjective experiences. It is important, also, to stand back from these and indicate what they show of you or how they fit with your life. It isn't enough just to produce feelings or images. Mulling over, the self-reflective part, comes when you ask why these now, what do they imply for me. Without this mulling over, the subjective becomes a forest of possibilities in which you are soon lost. You may want to question the very basis and nature of thought or experience itself. Sometimes you will be examining your values, what matters most to you, or where you take a stand. When having troubles with others, it would be well to examine your own reactions, attempt to formulate their position, and set an appropriate course of action. You may want to examine major issues such as war, love, politics, religion. In these areas it would be well to try to get at your own feeling-values to formulate your position. The scholarly or philosophical person may study a special interest such as art or language by considering the area through his own experiences.

Examples will clarify what I mean. The following begins with a fringe experience in which I try to describe just how my face felt. It leads, unexpectedly, to the discovery of a major personal trait. My judgment of the trait ends the entry.

My face, a mask of concern, worry, as though I seriously bore in and try to penetrate things. I could act carefree, but I don't choose to. My usual set is boring, penetrating concern to do what is right, best, perfect. Be a nice guy. Do your duties. Be so good no one can criticize. Sacrifice yourself first.

If I choose such a set, what reasons would I have? Well, in the first place, it seems defensive. Be so damn good no one can criticize. Yet they criticize me as being no fun, a worry-wort, which is correct. It is a prideful position, prideful over those who are not neat, punctual, doing things right. When I look at my do-good style it must be a pain in the ass to others! No wonder I have headaches. I delegate poorly ("Others won't do as well as I"). And it sure is a pain to me.

What commends such a style? I'm hard put to find anything. It wears me down and is unpleasant to others. It does little to protect from criticism and in part awakens it. I guess its greatest value to me is that I can feel that damn it, I tried. But this is somewhat like a plea to Nameless Fate, and Fate is not obliged to respond.

The following came after a visit to Karachi, Pakistan, as an officer on a ship. I had hired a cab driver to show me around. He asked me if I wanted hashish, women, or booze. He was a little surprised when I said I wanted to see how the masses of people live. The great poverty of the people bothered me. In Pakistan Allah is God and I felt a little angry at Allah. The entry is an effort to resolve this discomfort. It succeeds partially.

I've had two days of battling with language and money differences. Today I feel a sort of spiritual indigestion. The root of it is this terrible poverty. In this land I am a rich man able to give away rupees. Dirty kids, unwashed ragged clothes, no sidewalks, dirt, burlap hovels for homes. I visited a Moslem temple with mixed feelings. Rode a camel and felt a sudden burst of anger at Allah who keeps His people so poor.

I think a man has the right and, indeed, the obligation to question the works of Allah. But there is an equal obligation to try to see the use in what Allah does. I see a kind of alien justice buried in poverty. This by no means makes it right that it continue. Poverty wastes nothing, except perhaps people. In poverty everything is used. What man leaves, birds and insects eat. And what animals leave, time eats. And Allah eats time itself like a tidbit.

The following entry was made after having constant trouble with a superior officer on the ship. In a long prior section I analyzed his traits, but then decided there was something more I could learn from the situation.

More trouble with the chief mate today. It teaches me not to try to be the good guy with everyone. I am better off getting angry at him. Deeper—it teaches me to detach from interdependence on the opinions of some others. I'll never please him so to hell with him. Detach, so that in my life space I am stable and safe. It is my fault if I let him spoil my day. General Dictum—detach from those with whom there is no compatability.

The next entry illustrates self-reflection on borderline experiences leading to the experience of a trend that is the opposite of my usual consciousness. Again, the general direction was unclear until I had arrived.

There is a puzzling fringe to my present trend. Whatever I am doing —looking at my hand, listening to the clock tick—it says, "No, not there." This internal director pulls me away from the track, but toward what I don't know. I have a hunch that—an idea so vague it escapes me. It pulls me away from *any track!* Good heavens, I'll lose conscious direction! It leads me away from any fixity. I could, for instance, put my feet up on the desk and just stare at the wall. That would be okay to this new director. *Tracklessness.* It also would relieve me of all cares. It takes me away from things, from duties, from all must dos. It will accept any passing fantasy, or intuition or memory, willy-nilly, come what may. Of course, at the moment I am tracking tracklessness! With it comes all kinds of memories of times I did as I pleased. This tracklessness is a relief because I am so duty-bound. In a way it seems like the polar opposite of my consciousness.

Consciousness—I must do my duties, get ahead, not waste time—burden.

Other pole—drift, pin to nothing, do nothing, scatter, what the hell. Relief. Nothing to be done.

The reader may have sensed this to be a kind of self-analysis. Indeed successful self-analysis can proceed in this way, thus serving a number of functions. It studies, throws light on, and records any area of human experience. It may give life and substance to feelings or areas of human experience that are generally unknown or unrecognized. It clarifies what one believes and chooses. It forges a person.

For me a person, as distinguished from an average anybody, is one who has a distinctive style. He has reflected on his style. He can describe himself as others see him. He knows himself. Moreover, after reflection he has chosen to be as he is. He has a position. He takes a stand. He is unique, an individual. When I understand him, his style, his stand, his whole world is of one piece. It makes sense. He is not just a messy copy of others' opinions and ways. Such a person is interesting, like a complex drama with one rich thread of meaning running through it. Self-reflection forges of this kind of individuality.

What is self-reflection? Awareness. Awareness reaching round and searching its direction, its purpose, its source. It lies between psychology and philosophy and is higher than both. I consider this self-reflection one of the highest and most useful things a person can do. It raises a life of simply doing and responding to outside things to life imaging and judging itself. If nothing else, it makes use of all the subjective fringe of mind. It clarifies personal values. It enables one to judge and to plan. In my mind's eye I can see a state of being in which the whole of existence views itself, reflects on itself, becomes Aware of What Is. This is the place in the world above all the worlds.

If your journal lasts long enough to go into several volumes, you will discover that a few basic themes underly all of it. Moreover, these themes spiral around the root theme of your whole life. The root theme is often so universal, touching upon all things at once, as to be difficult to describe. It is as though all of life is a spiral searching its own core, and in the center is a peace that encompasses all and asks nothing further.

Summary

Self-reflection is how you look back on and question all aspects of your existence. It requires:

a. Minutes of leisure.

b. Experiencing what is. This can mean reflecting on external concerns, or looking inwardly at what arises.

c. Mulling it over. Reflect back on what you are doing and extract use from it.

To become a great contemplative:

a. Do it regularly, i.e., ten minutes every day.

b. Set it down in a private journal.

5

Feeling-Imagery

This continuity of love is what is called affection; and it is this
continuity that reigns in a man's life and makes all his delight, and
consequently, his very life; for man's life is nothing else but the
delight of his affection; and thus is nothing else but the affection of
his love. Love is man's willing, and derivatively is his thinking, and
thereby his acting.
Emanuel Swedenborg, *Arcana Coelestia* (¶ 3938), 1749–1756

Underlying the conscious processes of mind, which seem to be
under our direction, is a sea of feeling. This background is
forever capable of portraying our reactions to self and others
and of imaging forth our own inner trends. The sea of feeling
is relatively little known and neglected. We can only guess at
the reasons for this.

For one, we tend to identify mainly with the end-products of
mind: thought and action. From the relatively clear and differentiated viewpoint of thought and action, feeling looks like a
half-formed, indefinite, untrustworthy, slippery process. It
doesn't have the clear firmness of our verbal selves or our action

selves. It is too indefinite, dark, and unreliable.

Furthermore the verbal self, looking down on feeling, finds that it flees before the analysis of logic. It acts like a timid animal that prefers to hide from the presence of man-the-talker. Most of the rumors about the world of feeling are negative. People suspect feeling is perhaps just foolish and silly. It can be pushed any way one wants. The opposite kind of rumors about strong feeling are more ominous. With strong feeling a person may become uncontrollable or even dangerous. Perhaps we are all madmen and murderers at heart. Rumor can be backed by fact. Instances of crying or anger can be cited and shown to disturb the gentle flow of polite company. All told, reason decides it is the more fit to rule. Feeling is banished or restrained because either it is a weak, wishy-washy nothing, or it is too disruptive when it gets out of hand.

Going beyond rumor and myths of ourselves, feeling can soon be recognized as the background accompaniment of all perception, all thought, all action. The relaxed perception of this background allows our feeling to clarify its own meanings and direction. The key here is *relaxed perception,* which allows feeling to come forth and portray itself. Some people fear that they aren't experiencing real feeling—that they are making themselves feel whatever they want. This comes from a lack of acquaintance with this realm. The "what I want" itself comes from the realm of feeling. If encouraged to elaborate a fantasy a person soon finds he is merely blocking and redirecting feeling whenever it takes him into undesired areas. The longer the fantasy, the more it will tend to be governed by the inner direction of his own feelings. One man felt he could fantasize anything and thereby control all his inner directions. Because he looked quite masculine, I asked him to imagine he was an effeminate male dress designer. The fantasy had not gone very far before he was seducing his models, neglecting dress design, and forgetting he was effeminate. His own native inner direction crept in. At best the masterfully self-controlled individual tries to block certain trends in his inner feelings. The moment they arise, they are censored. Hence they arise again and again! The cure for the persistent fantasy is to go through it thoroughly.

Once in a small class on phenomenology a young woman implied that she had a dreadful fantasy that kept coming back. When I asked her about it she implied that it had to do with suicide. She didn't want to talk about it. I encouraged her to try it in the safe environment of the classroom. She was reluctant. She felt if the fantasy were allowed to express itself she would become actively suicidal. Finally she consented. In fantasy she got away from people and walked in the snow. She saw a deep snowbank. With fear and trembling she contemplated crawling into the snow to freeze to death. I encouraged her to go ahead. In her mind's eye she carved out an enclosed cavern in the snow. I asked her what it was like inside. She said, "Quiet! I hear no sounds of people." When asked she confirmed that she had had a bit much of people lately and wanted to get away from them. Then she chuckled and smiled. I asked why. She said she first thought the snow would be cold, but instead it reminded her of her own intense warmth. She felt snug and cozy inside the snow. I encouraged her to stay in it as long as she wanted and to return to it whenever she wanted to get away from people.

What at first sight seemed to her a deadly suicidal fantasy instead took on the meaning of a warm cozy place free from peoples and cares. She had not permitted herself such a respite. Hence the fantasy kept returning. Her misapprehension of the inner tendency as "Maybe I want to kill myself" was her misapprehension of her own inner tendency. When she found respite from people the whole suicidal idea disappeared. That is why it was important to emphasize that she could enter the warm respite of her snowbank any time she wanted to. Under similar circumstances others have killed themselves, having missed their own ever-handy fantasy snowbank.

The inner world easily draws together various aspects of experience in ways that would badly confound a rational philosopher bent on categorizing them. Inner perception expands into feeling. When intense enough, feeling can take off in fantasy with clear imagery. Thoughts can drift into feelings. Bodily sensations can easily be amplified into feeling-imagery. Our perception of others or of things can be relaxed into feeling-imagery. Self-reflection enters when we read back and understand our own inner drift. When we are accustomed to the process it should become easy to develop intense, detailed, colored fantasies right in the midst of washing the dishes or talking to a friend. Also, we can go back to an old fantasy at any time and watch its drift. In the same way we can walk again in childhood scenes.

Feeling has a drift. When allowed to drift, it intensifies as feeling-imagery. After it has been allowed to show its tendencies, one can then review the imagery to see what the inner direction is. With the woman in her snowbank, the inner drift was to get away from people and cares and snuggle up in a warm, cozy retreat. Having discovered the wisdom of one's own inner tendencies, one is then in a better position to cooperate with the underlying direction.

Some people fear that their own inner tendencies may not be wise; they may be too instinctual and animal-like and contrary to society. My own feeling is that such persons are caught up in rumors of the inner world. Experience with the inner world suggests that it may look strange and alien, but it is eminently wise. Rather than defend this thesis, let us look closer at its behavior.

The simplest use of feeling-imagery is to enlist its aid to see where one is at the moment. Since the whole sensory motor system of the body is its representative, one can dwell on bodily

60

feeling and come to an inner image and understanding of one's condition. For instance, while writing I feel like sitting back in my chair (relaxed perception) and twirling a horizontal pencil in my fingers. The right hand holds the point and turns it back and forth while the left hand feels the turning. I allow a fantasy to develop around this. I see an old water wheel mill. There are fascinating grinding and squeaking noises as the outer power of the water is converted through big crude wooden gears to revolving stone against stone where the grain is ground. The random power of the water that would otherwise have swept by is converted into the grinding of grain.

As I am writing this I slip and write gain instead of grain. The random water outside (feeling) is converted into awesome gear-turning and noises (images) to grind grain/gain (understanding). I feel the main point of both the turning pencil and the mill is the way power from one level is converted into work and change at another level. Of course I am trying to explain the way feeling converts thought. It is an old mill because this is an old process.

I am struck by the importance of the strength of the pencil in my hand. Because of its resistance to twisting, movement on one side is conveyed faithfully to the other side. This resistance to twist is our understanding and faith in this process whereby feeling does work in mind. Yet the source side—the fingers twirling the point—seems so much easier than the fingers feeling the rough metal end of the pencil. Similarly, in the image, the water is gentler than the grinding of the mill. Feeling is soft, easy, playful. The work of mind-intellect seems harsher, like the grinding.

An apparently spontaneous, random gesture was chosen by feeling to be its representative. By what I felt and noticed of the pencil turning, the inner feeling began to express its direction. By a little association with these sensations and perceptions I could read back the inner message coming forth. The fantasy of the mill was a parallel way of elaborating its direction. The process underlying my concerns was permitted to find its way into consciousness through an apparently spontaneous act (twirling the pencil), sensations from it, and by a parallel fantasy (the grist mill). But most remarkable of all, what I was trying to understand was trying to tell me of the nature of its own life. Our real concerns arise from this inner realm, and it is quite capable of speaking of them.

A good time to use this inner propensity is when one feels out of sorts or is caught in a mood. One should then stop, dwell on sensations, and allow them to amplify into a fantasy. A man is driving home from work with a headache.Having time while driving, he allows his physical sensations to speak up. When he dwells on it, the headache is more a stiffness down the back of the neck and shoulders. To grasp its meaning he portrays this stiffness. He holds his arms stiffly on the car's wheel. His shoulders and neck are rigid. His face feels as though it were in an angry scowl. The scene amplifies. He is on a battlefield. He has been mortally wounded.He is holding onto a tree stump. If he hangs on someone will come by and notice him and help him. The martyrlike hanging on in the image seems a bit humorous to the driver. In the image the wounded man smiles to himself and says, "Hell, an injured man is supposed to fall down." He relaxes, sits back in the car seat with his elbows in his lap. The man on the battlefield relaxes in the warm earth. He leisurely examines little plants springing up nearby out of the ruined earth of the battlefield. The driver concludes he has rigidly forced himself to do everything expected of him, secretly hoping someone would notice his plight and take pity on him. He notices himself, takes pity on himself, and allows himself to relax. Some stiffness in neck and shoulders remains. He concludes that next weekend he will take his family to the state park they want to visit.

By amplifying sensations into feelings and images he could

see better what he was doing. His "mortal wounds" came from driving himself too hard. The one that he hoped would notice and take care of him was himself. The torn-up battlefield and his injuries reflected the battle he had been through in the world of his work. The little plants springing up were the beginnings of new life as he relaxed and considered a trip to the state park. "Mortally wounded on the field of battle" sounds like a dramatic exaggeration. The inner life will use a very dramatic language to get its point across to the thick-headed individual. It does this in dreams too. You would do the same if you had to tell an individual what he was doing without words, by the use of imagery. Taken the other way around, the image was true, for in one sense the man was holding himself up though seriously wounded in life's battleground.

If you become accustomed to allowing feeling-imagery, you can use it to understand another person. At times I find it very difficult to describe what I see in a woman who is a stranger to me. I have a lot of vague unclear feelings. I allow these to elaborate into a fantasy. I'm going to have a date with her. Let's see how I feel a date with her should be handled. In one woman I feel I should be very modest about amorous advances. It would feel best if we visited a museum, went to dinner and a concert, and had much chance to talk of our ideas first. For another woman I feel we should go to a dance, be active, live it up. I've shared these fantasies with women in groups usually to find that they are amplifications of accurate perceptions of them.

Once, when studying a young man, all my impressions were crowded out by a fantasy. Suddenly he and I were in an alley in a poor neighborhood. He had a knife. I felt in danger. I shared this fantasy with him. To the surprise of all those present I was seeing the way he had lived most of his young life. He was a young tough in a ghetto neighborhood who carried a knife. At times onlookers have felt this was brilliant intuition or ESP on my part. For me it seems to be allowing vague impressions to express themselves as inner imagery.

Occasionally the process does seem to be extrasensory. I once interviewed a stout woman before a group. Immediately I saw a sharp, clear scene: a peaked-roof farmhouse on a flat plain, with a road coming up to it from the east. I could also see the life of the occupants: simple, barren, work. The emotional high points were meals together and Bible-reading sessions. I shared the image with the woman to see if she could find significance in it. It was a picture of her family home and of the essential quality of their life. Even the straight road coming in from the east was accurate. This appeared to be more than an elaboration of what I could see or knew of her. It is not too surprising. The evidence on extrasensory perception indicates it arises out of feelings and can express itself in images.

Such "miraculous" examples are not important, though. The main point is that one's unclear feelings can be expressed and clarified by a fantasy image of the other person. As with all observation, it should be checked out for accuracy, often just by asking the other person. Until its accuracy has been confirmed a number of times, no great decision regarding the other person should rest on such a process. There is always the chance that something of one's self is seen rather than the other person. In my own experience the image of another person that comes suddenly fully formed is usually accurate. Less accurate are the labored images that have more of my egotism involved in their formation.

It would be well if everyone simply practiced projecting himself into a random situation. This is perhaps the cheapest and one of the most effective psychotherapies, involving its basic elements. Allow yourself to be projected into a situation. Then read back the projection to learn what you can of yourself. The projection can be started on any object that catches the eye, or it may simply be spun out as an inner image. If an object is used,

64

there is more room for projection of the inner life if it is complex in form and hence has implications. This would be more true of clouds or plants than it would be of a pipe or chair. The object that catches your eye already has buried in it something of your own psychic tendencies. There is even more freedom to project if you spin out an inner image. To do its stunt, the inner life just needs a little time and freedom.

A very ordinary example will illustrate the process and will also suggest something of the complex wisdom of inner states. A young woman in her early twenties had come up through poverty, drug abuse, and eventually prostitution. She had become disgusted with her life and entered a difficult voluntary treatment program, which involved a great deal of encounter groups and peer pressure. She felt very mixed up in her values. Her main pattern had been to find an attractive man, seduce him, and depend on him. This had failed so often and so tragically that she couldn't go that way anymore, but she had not developed any new pattern of adjustment.

She was gazing at a random clump of plants on the green-carpeted floor. Most of the plants were new and green; a few were dead. A she looked at them she had a pervasive feeling of the dead ones. To her they looked ugly, barren, winter, terrible. Instead of fleeing this image, as most would have done at this point, she stayed with it. The clear impression came to her of the life going out of the plants. They were a mess. Leaves were crumpled up and dying. They would fall off. The whole thing would become simple stems. Spring would come sometime, but right now it was going through simple ugliness.

When she compared the image to her life she could see a number of similarities. All the insights she was gaining into her past behavior made her feel ugly. Unlike her old seductive self, she was neglecting her appearance and actually feeling ugly. The dropping leaves she related to dropping old attitudes and adjustments. Spring or the new way of life seemed far off. She was going through a dying winter decline. This she saw and accepted.

A few minutes later the whole scene had shifted. She could see herself walking slowly in a grassy meadow. There was no one else around. The green grass of the meadow was short, too short to hide in. She was pleased that she couldn't hide and pleased that no one else was around. Whatever she had to do, she would do herself. In the distance there were flowers, and the signs of richer life. She was in no hurry to get there. For the present it was enough to be alone in a simple green meadow.

Having accepted the dying, declining, losing of attributes in the first image, the second shows act two of her drama. There is some life in it (short green grass). The emphasis is on being alone, having to do it alone without possibility of hiding. As in the first image, life is promised in the future. It is closer to hand and more visible now (flowers and life can be seen from where she is). Everyone has opinions of what she is and how she should live. She was once very artful in seeming to comply with others' wishes; now she doesn't want to. Alone, in a place of some life (green grass), she is facing herself and working out her new values. The future is promising; flowers and other life are within reach now.

When she began exploring her image she only knew she felt bad. Being caught up in the dying barrenness of the plants almost caused her to shut off the inner imagery. The dying plants were exactly where she was then. Even in appearance she was allowing herself to look ugly partly to get away from the old values of the seducer. *If one stays with the inner process it tends to be therapeutic.* By facing up to her own dying, changing, simplifying, the inner drama can advance to the next stage. Though the rational mind is inclined to think these things have to take time, the inner is more free of time. The next act came suddenly in a wholly different image while looking at the same plants. This image had the same implication of simplicity (plants becoming twigs in the first image, a plain meadow in the second). But further keys were given in the second. She must do it alone. It was important that she not be able to conceal herself any longer. It was a simple facing of herself that had in it more life (green grass) and a nearer promise of future improvement (flowers and life in sight). The two images were a clarification of what she was beginning to feel was the direction for her to take.

In groups she thanked others for advice on how she should live, but she said she really felt she had to work it out for herself for a while. As a seducer she had always become entangled in the needs and wishes of others. The new woman was becoming more independent. The whole fantasy reflected and helped make conscious where she was at the moment, the method by which she could solve her situation, and how close she was to getting out of it. This is a good deal to get from looking at a simple bunch of plants. Yet this process is available to anyone, at any time.

It should be a matter of some importance as to how the inner life portrays itself so accurately. This issue will arise again and again in this book. The inner life has this capacity; this is its most fundamental characteristic. It shares the life of the individual and is concerned about the quality and direction of that life. I thinks of its situation in very feeling-laden, dramatic life terms. It readily portrays the individual's over-all goals and direction. It is even able to suggest how an individual can get out of what binds him. The analytical psychologist Carl Jung called these processes the objective unconscious. They are far more objective than the individual about the direction of his life. Consciousness is certainly limited. The objective unconscious may not be limited. The perspective of the feeling background on the life of the individual is considerably greater than that of the conscious individual.

Yet the inner life intrudes very little into the freedom of the individual's will. For the most part it stands in the wings, waiting to be summoned. In obsessive thoughts, compulsive acts, and psychosis, one begins to see some intrusion of the inner life into conscious experience. Persistent moods are also a kind of intrusion. It is as though the inner apparently leaves the individual free so long as he is working out the general direction of the inner life. The more he fails, the more it begins to stand forth and take a hand. What we see as mental illness represents the inner more manifestly taking a hand in the individual's life. It will live whether or not the individual permits it. When the individual merely tries to cooperate with the inner, it is a most powerful ally—his only real ally. If the individual's own understanding and self-conception is too limited, it will send diverse signals and guides. Unfortunately most individuals overlook these. Finally the inner life protrudes into his life like a sore thumb and he looks emotionally disturbed or mentally ill. It is a wry bit of humor to think that most minds fail to understand their own nature.

The idea of freedom in this context is not so simple. The individual feels free and acts most free when he accurately represents his inner tendencies. Freedom and doing what he feels like doing are much the same. And what a person feels like doing is to act as the embodiment of his inner trends. The felt degree of freedom diminishes as he goes against the inner trends. Psychosis is an ultimate example of what happens when a person acts thoroughly against his inner or natural trends. It is not as though we are free to be the slaves of the inner. The inner is the real substance and nature of our lives. We simply are not free to turn against it.

In light of this, all occasions in which things aren't going well are very appropriate points at which to project feeling-images, then try to read back what they mean to you. To read them back I usually ask individuals, "How is this like your life?" People can feel connections with their life when they can't begin to explain the images that came to them. Explanation, the clever operations of reason, are *not wanted*. They are themselves a severe impediment to understanding the signals from within. It is far better that the individual try in however limited a fashion to feel how the image seem like his life. Even a relatively stupid feeling out of one's own images is better than reason or the guess of the best outside experts. Outsiders are inclined to project their own lives into one's own images. Occasionally I have seen very good friends make meaningful guesses about an another's images. But you are the life that projects your images. Your most halting understanding is closer to its own source. Also, your understanding is as far as you can get at the moment. The inner process is exceedingly tolerant of any effort to understand it. It can issue forth dreams, fantasies, images forever until you understand that which is the basis of your understanding.

In general the inner is concerned with the whole quality and style of your life. It is not very involved in whether you take this job or that job, etc., unless the jobs feel very different and represent fundamentally different approaches to life. The inner will talk about directions you are now taking or contemplating, but it is rarely predictive. If you want it to comment on what stocks to buy, it is more likely to kid you about the foolishness of your aims. Though it may know the future, it rarely shows it. It is more like a psychotherapist or a very good friend. Its fundamental concern is with the design and quality of your life, not in making you rich or famous. And it is in the design and quality of your life that it is a master consultant. The fact that this consultant doesn't speak an ordinary language is also an advantage. It speaks in dramatic feeling-terms of life. One must feel into the language to understand it. That is, one must become more like this source of information to understand it.

As one works with feeling-images it may well become apparent that one has entered a new realm of time that is little understood. A single dramatic theme can stand in the background of one's life for a whole lifetime, awaiting expression. The critical childhood traumas that psychoanalysts used to find are examples of this. In a similar way individuals may have whole sets of values in the background, waiting for expression. In subtle and little-understood ways these background propensities effect choice and behavior. These timeless propensities can wait forever, or come forth and change in short order. It is as though they can change only by coming through one's life. If the background tendency implies suicide, weird perversions, etc., we are inclined to keep them from expression. Yet when lived out in fantasy they can change in a few moments. One woman was afraid she was homosexual because she wanted to look at women's figures. I suggested that she look all she wanted in fantasy. The inner wish to look went from legs to breast to her being cuddled like an infant by an older woman. She had been raised without a mother and really wanted to experience being mothered. The real meaning and drift of the inner cannot be understood until lived out in some way. Fantasy is safe. In it one can slay thousands, die, and be born again all in a space of a few minutes. The inner is permanent and timeless when unlived. When lived out it advances the individual through acts of a very well-conceived drama. The greatness of the inner plot may be apparent only when looking back on a lifetime of experience.

It is also possible to intensify the relationship to the inner process by trying to cooperate in reasonable and socially acceptable ways with its aims. The overworked man with a stiff neck resolved to take his family on an outing. This was a clear acceptance of the inner message and an attempt to comply with its implied direction. One man looked at a plant leaf and saw a dog he had run over years before. He had driven by, saying to himself, "To hell with it." Now the dog was back, dying again. The elaborated fantasy implied that his fault lay not in the accidental killing of the dog, but in his careless regard for the mess he had made. He respectfully buried the leaf as though it were the dog, thereby completing a scene that had lain a long while in the background of his thought. This sounds like a very primitive response. Yet the man had wisely moved in the direction of his own inner bent. A tiny bit of understanding and cooperation with one's own natural bent goes a long way.

Summary

1. The inner life comes forth easily with the patient, relaxed perception of what is suggested by things before one or directly in inner imagery.

2. With practice this capacity can be greatly intensified until one can see detailed colored scenes at any time.

3. These are reflections of the inner life.

4. To learn from this process one needs to feel into the dramatic language of the inner life in order to read back how it reflects one's self.

5. The central concern of the inner life is the meaning and quality of one's life.

6. The process seems timeless until it can be expressed in one's life in some way. Reasonable efforts to comply with inner directions greatly advances the unraveling of their implications.

7. This process can be used to

(a) interiorize bodily sensations to learn what one's own body has to say.

(b) clarify impressions of another person through fantasy.

(c) portray a mood so as to understand better the message of the mood.

(d) project one's inner values and tendencies to see better what one's natural inclinations are.

Unlocking and using this inner capacity is perhaps the briefest effective therapy one can do for one's self.

In the Stillness of Mind

What is actually the first effect of life is inmost thought, which is the perception of ends.
Emanuel Swedenborg, *Divine Love and Wisdom* (¶ 2), 1763

That which a man has as the end is plainly discerned, for it reigns universally in him; and thus is continually present even at those times when he seems to himself not to be thinking at all about it, for it is seated within and makes his interior life, and thus secretly rules each and all things.
Emanuel Swedenborg, *Arcana Coelestia* (¶ 5949), 1749–1756

Anyone who has made a real effort to penetrate the operations of mind discovers at one time or another the need to still and limit its operations. The reason is simple. The normal flow of mental experiences is too rich to understand fully any little aspect. Most of the efforts at stilling the mind have been called meditation. Since the mind cannot be stopped, these efforts have centered on focusing and limiting its operation. When this is done, some of the underlying bases of mind's functioning become more apparent.

That mind cannot be stopped is not immediately apparent to some. Mind and experiencing are the same. To stop the mind would be tantamount to saying: do not experience. You shut off sight by closing the eyes, only to become more aware of sound. With eyes closed in a soundless room one becomes very aware of bodily sensations. If one floats fetal-like in body temperature water, one soon intensely experiences inner imagery as the experiments in sensory deprivation show.[1] One cannot shut off this very lively inner experiencing except by falling asleep. Then one wallows into dreams. There may really be blank periods in between the eight or so dreams one has every night, but they are difficult to examine.[2] Once I was repeatedly lowered into profound unconsciousness by an anesthetist using a nitrous oxide and oxygen mixture.[3] At the lowest stage of unconsciousness, in which breathing itself stopped, I had tremendous cosmic experiences that I was very disappointed to leave by someone breathing me back to life. Other than possible blank spells in sleep, the mind can't really be turned off. I have long speculated that chronic schizophrenics, who seem to have screened out most of the normal social world, ought to have hallucinations and delusions from this sensory isolation alone. The mind will always fill up with something. If given nothing to fill it, it fills itself.

Direct efforts to still the mind by focusing it on something usually begin by making one aware of the way in which mind wanders off like a willful donkey. Through the centuries men have chosen a great variety of ways of focusing mind. Some concentrate on a part of the body such as the middle of the forehead or on breathing. Some add words by counting their breath or saying "in-out" with each breath. Some gaze at a very simple point. Others try to focus on simple repetitive sounds (the mantra) or a repeated single sound. For some the position of the body is critical.[4] One must be in zazen, cross-legged with hands in the lap. Each way of focusing has been raised to the level of a school with adherents and detractors. Westerners who try zazen often find it a painful muscle-stretching experience, not the easy relaxed position intended by Oriental masters. It is excellent if one wants to meditate on pain!

There are some simple considerations if one wants to focus the mind to expose some of its underlying operations. If one gets too comfortable one may fall asleep. It was said tea was invented to keep the Zen masters awake. Hence practitioners have tended to adopt some kind of sitting-up position. For the same reason it may be important to keep the eyes open rather than closed. A safe beginning is with eyes open, comfortably sitting up, gazing at a tiny spot. To remove the distraction of random noises one could meditate on these sounds with eyes closed. In time the formerly distracting sounds will produce ideas and later inner imagery, much as they do in dreams. One can also fixate on a part of the body, on breathing, or on the heartbeat. To begin, gazing at a spot is recommended.

Those who haven't spent hours meditating may well wonder why people bother. Those who have spent even twenty minutes a day meditating over a period of months are visibly different. They seem calmer, integrated, all together. It is as though they collected themselves and they remain collected. Their bodily movements are smoother, less hasty, more balanced. On inquiry they show considerable sensitivity, both inward and outward. Their knowledge of inner experience is noticeably beyond the average. Practice at stilling the mind lends peace to the individual. It also intensifies inner processes so that the individual can embark on a free self-analysis. It is a very intimate kind of learning because one isn't verbally talking about experiences but is working within experience itself. Also, stilling the mind gives one a refuge that can always be entered. I remember in one bitter life experience I was also meditating on the beauty of flames in the fireplace. Much of psychic disorder seems to stem from the psyche feeling it has no real alternatives. It must work out *this* problem, whatever it is. Meditation opens up alternate worlds as valid as that of one's painful problems.

Meditation is quite closely related to dealing with feeling-images. While heading in the same general direction as when working with feeling, it involves a greater focusing and limiting of the attention with a consequent increase in spontaneous inner processes. Meditation exposes more of the underlying nature of human experience itself.

The possible discoveries from meditation can be arranged in a rough series. Your first experiences are likely to illustrate how unruly the mind is. When you try to fix on a spot, all kinds of ideas may go through your head. You will find yourself asking, "Why am I doing this? When can I quit? I should be doing some work, etc." You will also discover a host of itches and intruding sensations. If you identify with the statements that call you away from meditation, you soon quit. Or you can let them go by like the comments of some impatient stranger. You don't have to identify with everything said in your head! The itches are a more fundamental resistance. If you don't scratch them, your first meditation can focus around the agonies of itching. Scratch the worst of them, but don't let the stubborn animal within get away with too much.

As you get into meditation, the mind, finding itself bereft of the usual garbage that occupies it, begins playing like a child. Your attention wanders from this to that aspect of the spot you are focused on. Gradually meanings are suggested. At this level you are close to what is experienced in feeling-images. For a long while the mind will skip around from an extraneous sound, to an itch, to implied meanings in the spot, to tiring of the eyes, etc. You may wrestle with the issues in this skipping around. You may wonder if you make the skipping. Generally the answer is no. As the restless mind tires of one aspect it lights on anything else handy. It is almost like an animal desperate to be occupied. If you look closely you may find it is almost impossible to trace the fading of interest in one thing before another replaces it. In fact, you may find you just went through a blankness only after you suddenly realize you are focused on a new aspect. There is a pattern: noticing one thing, fading interest, blankness, new interest emerging, sudden realization you lost the old focus. You may also flash back and forth between sensory or inward awareness and rediscovery of the spot. This is the beginning of a number of discoveries that suggest the operations of mind are much more spontaneous than we normally suspect.

There are a number of sensory changes that can emerge. You notice different aspects of the spot: it can move, become something not seen before, change color, and even disappear. This goes along with a successful focusing on a visual stimulus. Then it will vary the stimulus itself. These variations take on more and more dramatic meaning as though the spot were beginning to perform. It should take relatively little effort at this point to understand how the performance is related to your own life, for, after all, the performance is made out of your nature. If the performance gets lively enough you can even inwardly ask the spot questions and have it enact answers. At this point the results of meditation are rich enough to hold the attention to the spot.

Along the way a long battle may develop over how all this is controlled. You may wish to adopt one attitude and find its opposite reigning. You may want to keep the mind focused, yet it wanders so cleverly. You may even want to divest yourself of willfulness only to find you are being so willful about it. This is perhaps the most difficult rock and shoal of meditation. Things go much easier if you learn early that the inner processes have a will of their own and simply follow that will to learn from its direction. There are several alternatives in meditation if you have the problem of unwilling will. Don't identify with acts of will. For instance, if you find yourself saying, "I don't want to control this," don't identify with this willful statement. Even the effort not to will is willful. Willing, choosing, deciding, can be split away as autonomous processes that happen and drift by. Another way out is to exhaust the will. If willfulness can't be let go of, then use it ruthlessly until it is worn out. Some sail by the rocks of willfulness easily because they enjoy watching the inner drift of mind and never particularly want to control it.

There are also several pleasant plateaus of experience you can stumble upon. There is the discovery that meditation is a world of its own and that it can be returned to any time not only as a refuge, but to gain perspective on the outer world. In this state you may enjoy long periods of just feeling pleasant and peaceful. From this perspective thoughts of the outer world may seem rather distant and unreal. It is possible to review your behavior in that outer world and feel it was unnecessarily frantic or foolish. At this point the mind has become tame to the centering process itself. It no longer balks at focusing as it did at first. Related to this plateau are pleasant discoveries about time itself. The formerly inexorable clock-ticking time may languidly spread out and discover its own peace. Hours can become moments or moments hours. Time becomes stretchable and quite relative. Time itself may disappear as a useless issue.

After the mind is tamed to focus, it then playfully lays out a number of possibilities that gradually knit into a general understanding. Here the power of the inner message begins to carry over into your life. Life experience is not just another harsher world now; it is one of the components of meditation, the component in which you try out new insights.

The above experiences are sufficient reason for meditation. Yet within meditation it is possible to achieve a much higher state that has become the main goal for some.[5] This has variously been called enlightenment, satori, moksha, and other terms. It comes at first as a very brief experience of seeing into the nature of things. At higher levels there are periods of a loss of self-identity and a sudden awareness of the total nature of creation. The higher levels of this experience are relatively rare. It would be well not to bend all one's efforts to attain this kind of breakthrough because effort certainly does delay its appearance. It would be wiser to enjoy and master all the lower levels of meditation first. Satori is more likely to occur where the individual has come to understand himself in depth. And this understanding of the self in depth is sufficient reason in itself for meditation.

Many of these points will be illustrated by a young man's early experience in meditation. He was gazing at a white spot on the lacquered plywood floor of his basement study. The spot looked about three-eighths of an inch long, roughly circular, elongated in the upper left, having a tail in the lower left.

I examined it for some while, noting its features. It seemed to have a slight thickness, it was clear against its surroundings. It seemed I could hear myself trying to describe its features, and then realized that words were not adequate. I could retire into a deeper level of appreciation of its features, leaving behind words. It seemed the whole territory of how well words fit things could have been explored, but was left behind. Later, features first unnoticed would become prominent. For instance a faint highlight in its whiteness grew intense for a time. It became apparent that it could not be seen all at once, but only gradually, and as far as I explored new features continued to emerge in the visible features of my simple spot.

I could withdraw into awareness of seeing itself, as though seeing were a cone projected from me to go to the spot, surround it, and bring it back to me. It then became apparent that around the fringe of any simple experience I could find imagery or fantasy, and that this served to amplify and clarify what would have been a vaguer perception. The cone cast out to bring the spot to me was one example. Or I could gaze at the spot and withdraw into awareness of my facial muscles. A mild pain from a sinus attack was amplified in a fantasy as though the bones around my eyes and forehead obtruded like a Cro-Magnon man. There was a kind of heavy, sullen, irritable, cavemanlike feeling. This was an amplification of an attitude I often found in myself.

Often my mind would go away from the spot. Sometimes I found myself preparing lectures or doing other things and felt annoyed, restless, and bored. The valence of the spot was still less than my other concerns! It was as though I were pulled away into other things and the spot vanished even while looking at it. This kind of experience led me to ask myself how much I ran this process, but the question was too much to answer at first. My mind wandered from its impossibility. But I did have the impression that my awareness was made and cast out without my knowing how.

Within the gazing at the spot there was some feeling of relief at being safe within this simplicity and escaping the stream of worrisome events. When I was with the spot, much else was not. Its simple unde-mandingness was a respite.

Suddenly sounds emerged. At first I put them in their places—i.e., that is a sound of a clock in the next room, those are foorsteps over-head. This naming and placing them as "other" left them as intruders into my gaze. By relaxing attention it was also possible to hear the sound emerge from the spot. Faintly at first and clearer later, these spot-emitted sounds awakened vague images of color. Along with this colored sound, there were intimations of meaning beyond my grasp. After one wandering of attention from the spot I determined to hold myself to it and faintly heard the word "flog." This captured the feeling of whipping myself by holding myself to the task. This was another whole realm I could have explored in my spot, but chose not to.

There were several periods of altered perception. The spot would blur and almost disappear from prominence, usually with a concomi-tant awareness of my inner experiences. There was one period where I watched purple wavelike images form, sweep to the periphery, and disappear repeatedly. I knew my attention was weakened and rhyth-mic sensory processes could come into the foreground.

Suddenly the spot was obviously a fetus with a bloated belly and too small a head. This struck me as an image of my situation at that mo-ment. I was fetal, at the beginning of my understanding of this experi-ence. The bloated belly reminded me of my feeling rich, being con-cerned with my weight, and feeling I have much riches within. The small head represented my weak understanding.

A distant dog's bark turned into a long tubular corridor with the bark lining and forming the walls. It indicated something with dark blank-ness at the end I didn't understand. Here was sound, image, and repre-sentation rolled into one, signifying the presence of something I didn't yet understand, like the fetal spot before me. I wanted to. Suddenly

I noticed a little hand on the left-facing fetus. This felt like it meant (I) want to do (hand) but am not yet able to (little hand, little head, fetal). The fetus and its swollen stomach suggested it was pregnant with possibilities.

To my surprise the corridor, which was difficult to see, now came easily. A little reflection suggested that it was an everted image of my own mind. Its lower part was a dark band reminding me of despairing feeling. The upper left was bright like hope. Its whole form had complex suggestions. The empty end suggested that reality itself was empty. The corridor was my thought itself, with despair and hope leading to the peace of emptied-out reality. There was a satisfying warm feeling as though this was what I should be doing. I wondered if this couldn't be done with eyes closed, but I tended to fall asleep.

I tried to grasp what was cast out of me—the process of perceiving itself—and suddenly the spot was clearly a beaver turning to the left (association, the unconscious) to set to work (beaver, work). He looks well fed (similar to earlier associations to the stomach), needing to gnaw (verbalize), swim (intuit), and build a dam (write a paper). The motion and intent of the beaver was in the foreground, and in the background were the above associations of meaning.

Again I attempted to understand how this was cast out from me and returned to me as my perception and understanding. It occurred to me that what I called myself was this self-determined process of experiences. That it was determined or had a course of action I took as my own determination as though I owned it and made it so. Yet it was determined or had a course of action without my effort. Its determination owned me. The me or self looked like a fiction of its determination.

Now the beaver chewed fiercely as though he needed to use his teeth (and this needed to be expressed). Suddenly the scene was different. It became a *picture* of an active beaver, its jaws agape as though time stood still. Looking into the darkness of the jaws it was as though action, by being represented in a still picture, was belied by its opposite. Here was time, the picture of action, in stillness—represented and belied by its opposite. Time itself seemed a fiction. I could examine the busy beaver in detail in this still picture. All the Oriental statues of Buddha and other gods took on a new meaning. The still statue was not a representation, it was life in stillness, or all the vagaries of life undone and dominated by the more fundamental stillness of eternity. Action and time itself were the images of this stillness. The beaver's teeth were razor-sharp triangles representing the fierce dangers inherent in time-boundedness. Yet, while there was endless threat in the jaws, they would never close.

When I withdrew into inner perception the beaver turned left toward me and was about to bite its own tail like uroboros*. Here the meaning was essentially as before. Stillness imaged itself as about to seize itself, creating the circle of time. This was like the black empty center of my corridor lined with the bark of a dog (an action). Change was an appearance in changelessness. I could examine the peaceful black pupil of the snarling beaver's eye. It seemed as though all sounds came from his eye. The white spot was a reflection of light on the dark pupil. The light of the world was external to the warm comfortable feeling of the dark eye.

Now the beaver was the small one leading away from me. I grew restless and wanted to discontinue this exercise and do other things (i.e., I am led away toward things). The beaver turned away and I did too. I came away from meditation feeling I had seen more of the meaning of time and existence than I could understand.

The above meditation took only twenty minutes. The subject experienced a number of changes in the simple spot he observed. He passed by several realms he could explore—changing sensory impressions of the spot, his own face and bodily reaction, how much he controlled the experience, etc. The greatest drama occurred when the spot suddenly became a fetus that seemed to him to represent his then weak understanding. The earlier cone of vision reappeared as an image of his mind with several moods on the surface but ultimately emptied out of reality. This image implied more than he could understand. His effort to grasp it became a busy beaver who actively represented his state. Then the beaver became time frozen, an image of activity or life in an eternal stillness. This was also the implication of the empty cone as a representation of his mind. He could explore eternal quiet sameness and see

*An ancient symbol of a circle formed by a snake biting its own tail. Its many meanings include what is uncreated, creating out of itself, and appearing to devour itself. The empty circle formed by it has the implication of changelessness, the eternal.

82

on it a representation of activity (i.e., the beaver's biting jaw that would never close). He could experience change as just an appearance in changelessness.

Why this drift to his meditation? He was very interested in mysticism and comparative religion. What arose out of him was a surprising seeing of time from eternity. In later sessions similar themes would come back with even clearer representations as his understanding grew. The inner process instructed him in the general direction of his interests.

When the mind is stilled to look at its own processes, it tends to represent its own state in various ways such as bodily sensations, thoughts, images, spontaneous words, perceptions, and the emergence of meaning. When looked at closely in these representations of itself, it tends to lead beyond itself into an over-all understanding of reality.

7

Fragile Fringe Phenomena

... There is thought which is interior and more interior, also exterior and more exterior. What is actually the first effect of life is inmost thought, which is the perception of ends. But of all this hereafter, when the degrees of life are considered.
  Emanuel Swedenborg, *Divine Love and Wisdom* (¶ 2), 1763

In our gradual descent into the natural depth in man we now enter an area that is less understandable than what came before. We went from the external aspect of one's perceptions of others to the more conscious processes of mind to processes that gradually become more feeling-laden and symbolic. Now we pass through a region that is among the least understood. It is also one of the more difficult regions from which to get data. Some of the phenomena from this region are so little known they do not even have a name.

  One general tendency of our descent into mind has been to move away from conscious ego control. The phenomena to be described here are just over the conscious/unconscious border. While traces of ego are involved, it is mostly as an observer of quite spontaneous and autonomous processes within.

Most of what is to be described are phenomena from the hypnogogic state. Even some psychologists do not know of this state. Hypnogogic phenomena arise when one is lying down, very relaxed and nearing sleep. The general sequence of events as one approaches this state can be described. First one lies down and becomes comfortable. Worries from the day and sensations from the bed are mixed for a while. One may choose to center on a favorite fantasy. Gradually the mind slips out of gear. Stray images and phrases float through one's head. Yet one is still awake enough to note these if one chooses to make the effort. The individual can watch relatively spontaneous unconscious processes bubble to the surface. Most people lazily fall into a fantasy and walk off into a dream and sleep. It requires unusual persistence to stay poised between sleep and waking. Few have done it, and those who have tried it lost a lot of sleep. Yet they found a new and complex realm of possibilities, which will be seen to be an extension of what was beginning to appear in meditation. There is a great deal of symbolism in this area. It is perhaps all symbolism.

To my knowledge there are only a few great explorers who have recorded their observations in this area. Oddly enough, one of the earliest explorers in this region made the richest and most complex discoveries. Moderns seem far less daring and poorer equipped to deal with autonomous symbolic processes. Swedenborg has done more work in this area than anyone else. He approached this region by focusing inwardly and breathing minimally in the style of Raja Yoga. At first he wanted to focus all his powers of concentration to think better. As shown in his *Journal of Dreams* and *Spiritual Diary*,[1] he soon saw he was watching the raw natural processes of the mind at work. This region is immensely symbolic, and he learned to penetrate symbols from this experience.[2] Incidentally he broke through from the hypnogogic state into a personal journey through heaven and hell, and he left a profound and fascinating account of his discoveries.[3] Even very average people who explore this region can run into strange people and strange symbolic conversations that look like visitations from another world. In more modern times the French existentialist Jean-Paul Sartre also spent many hours exploring the hypnogogic.[4] Sartre missed the great key to understanding this region that had been understood by Swedenborg and found again later by Herbert Silberer.[5] The region is naturally autosymbolic, that is, it represents where one is at the moment. Or, put another way, it represents itself.

Much of the hypnogogic area looks simply like cute images and odd sentences being tossed around in one's head until one asks precisely what the individual was thinking of at that same moment. Then it begins to look like either a representation of the person's state or an answer to his query. Examples will clarify this autosymbolic character of the state.

I was trying to pick up hypnogogic experiences and heard, "Still a nothing." I wasn't getting much and it said as much. While I was trying to see in detail how the hypnogogic experience forms I heard, "Do you have a computer?" I was getting very sleepy in the hypnogogic state and heard, "The usual snoofing." At the time the odd word "snoofing" sounded like a cross between snooping (trying to snoop on the hypnogogic) and snoozing (getting sleepy). It was a playful representation of where I was—both snooping and snoozing.

In the hypnogogic there isn't much doubt that one has run into something alien to normal mental processes. The images arise suddenly and are fully formed before one can even guess what they imply. Similarly, a person can hear sentences or phrases that are not immediately understood. The process requires some study to find meaning in it. Even with concerted effort one may be able to trace sense in only a portion of what turns up. For instance, in the same night I picked up the above comments I also heard someone say, "Master, you are playing

86

games with me." Later someone said with great determination, "It does with me!" It was as though I had broken into someone else's conversation. I couldn't connect it with my state at the moment, but that may have been because it passed so fast. Even when the hypnogogic is obviously being autosymbolic of one's state at the moment, it is just of that precise instant. A fraction of a second later what it is representing may have passed. But the above phrases were quite beyond my understanding. That same evening I heard the hypnogogic saying, "I didn't want anything to happen to my sphere so I read Chekhov. Your sphere will have a repair letter on it." I have no idea why this conversation occurred, though it is intriguing. These spoken phrases are usually said in the tone of your own voice. It is surprising at first to see your mind thinking and talking without your bidding. When you say something to yourself the meaning is there before it is said. When something is said in the hypnogogic, or an image is experienced, the meaning is not there. It may take considerable work even to find its possibility.

My suspicion is that the hypnogogic and psychotic hallucinations are closely related. There is the same alien quality of an image or a sentence suddenly appearing out of nowhere, leaving one guessing as to why. There are differences, though. Hallucinations are much more vivid. Psychotics can literally and clearly see and hear things while awake. Normals, with considerable effort, have difficulty picking up these trace experiences while nearly asleep. Also, auditory hallucinations in psychotics are usually not in their own voice. My guess is that the psychotic, being more alienated from his own nature, experiences the same general processes as more intense and in a more alienated form.

The general nature of this inward terrain can be described. The way to the hypnogogic state is to lie down and relax as though going into sleep. One might direct attention to the eigenlicht, the vague, half-apparent colored lights and images seen with eyes closed. These are also called the entoptic or idioretinal lights. With concentration on them they can become clearer and clearer images. The patterns swirl, move, constantly change. With an intensifying of inner awareness they can form into simple objects or geometric patterns, sometimes in complex over-all designs. One I've often seen is formed out of delicate fern leaves. If one awakens slowly from sleep one may be able to linger on half asleep, looking at a wholly formed scene. A common one for me is a shore line of city lights. These inner eigenlichts seem impossible to hold still. My guess is that the brilliantly colored background imagery one may hallucinate under the drug LSD or other hallucinogens is simply an amplification of the normal eigenlicht. The meaning of the eigenlichts is quite unknown, since few people have examined them. My guess is that they too are autosymbolic of one's state. Seeing geometric patterns goes with a more analytical set. My own fern-leaf designs seem to go with a very peaceful languid state, the feeling suggested by ferns growing in shaded areas. The eigenlichts seem to be the bare beginning of inward self-representation.

To my knowledge, another phenomenon in this area has not been described before. When nearly asleep I find myself locked into some kind of logical relationship. There may be a fixed image and I go over the logic within its form repeatedly. I have the impression it is like a perfectly balanced, very complex, logical presentation. When I awaken it is difficult to remember, though. I may come out with some very paradoxical statement. When, within it, all its logical relationships seem perfectly clear although complex and often paradoxical. I have the feeling it is gone over repeatedly to get it fixed in the mind, yet it fades rapidly on full awakening. My own inner tendency and deepest need is to understand things. A common fantasy is that I am giving a very complex and well-presented lecture. My guess (and this is clearly an area of guess and uncertainty) is that this

88

unnamed kind of instructive logical process is autosymbolic of my own tendencies. I badly need a total understanding of a whole system. Left to its own devices, my mind seems to fall into such understandings. Others, with other tendencies, may well have a parallel kind of process going on in them. My wife, a woman of native good humor, falls into a humorous situation as she goes to sleep. I can tell by her mumbled chuckle that she has fallen asleep.

A rough descriptive map of the hypnogogic realm can be drawn. It is clearest in the state between sleeping and waking. Both sides must be present. One is totally relaxed and approaching sleep so inner processes can become more conscious. But one is awake enough to observe them. It occurs on the way into or out of sleep. If one awakens part way, it is quite easy to observe hypnogogic phenomena until one becomes so awake as to knock them out. *The main advantage of this difficult balancing act between sleeping and waking is that the conscious person can observe an indeed even talk to and experiment with inner process!* Examples of this will be given later. This state has the advantage over fantasy and meditation in that one can be sure one is not generating the actual responses of the hypnogogic state. Usually these are autonomous, i.e., the images and what was said are not immediately understood.

There is no question that the hypnogogic area is difficult to deal with in contrast to the states already described. One easily falls off to sleep. On the other hand, if one is too wakeful, it is easy to block it. This is the first major lesson to be learned. The hypnogogic comes spontaneously in little quick images or things said. If one instantly alerts and tries to retain it, this much ego can block any further appearance of it. It may take weeks or months to learn to relax enough to continue to observe the hypnogogic without blocking it by an excess of ego. *Very clearly it is the antithesis of ego.* Where ego is absent, it can appear. One of the several values in developing an ability to observe hypnogogic phenomena is in learning to lay aside ego, learning ego's deleterious effect in inner processes. Often it is difficult to remember. Like a dream it fades fast on awakening and getting into normal activity. If you can dictate into a tape recorder when half asleep you can capture a good deal of it. The eigenlicht, images with eyes closed, hypnogogic, and dreams could well be a single continuum in which ego fades and the inner awakens. Dreams seem longer and more intense experiences than these forerunners. The person is usually in his dream but is more of an observer of the hypnogogic.

For most people the hypnogogic is primarily visual, for some primarily auditory.[6] This same kind of division will later be found in psychotic hallucinations. It is not known yet why these differences exist. It could have something to do with the way one enters the process (i.e., concentrating on the eigenlicht, making it visual, or listening for voices). Or it could reflect basic personality differences. Perhaps those more extroverted and sensation-oriented see things and those more introverted and of intuitive bent hear things. The images can be black and white or in color. My guess is that the more intense the process the more likely it is to be in color. All other senses can appear too, i.e., taste, physical sensations, etc. One young man in a hypnogogic state felt hit with a solid object that struck him in the head, made his ears ring and muscles contract, and he felt faint. This particular experience was easily remembered because it was so intense.

Even though it is a difficult state to achieve and explore, it has its own lessons. It is my vague impression that there are levels of the hypnogogic state itself, which seem to have to do with how well one understands and deals with the process. As one enters into it better, its own apparent richness and power seems to grow. This may be an extension of the general idea that the main thrust of inner processes seems to be autosymbolic; the processes may reflect not only one's state, but also one's understanding and capacities.

Material roughly illustrative of these levels will help clarify something of both the levels and power of the hypnogogic. When one first runs into the hypnogogic it seems to be just a lot of random firings of the brain, bits of images and phrases. I have seen faces I couldn't recognize and heard comments in the background. I wasn't sure if I were overhearing bits of conversation or hearing bits of my own thoughts.

Upon closer examination it appears rather clearly autosymbolic. I was thinking of the richness of the process and heard, "My liberal arts course." While meditating on a pain in my head I heard, "Nonmaterial!" Of course the experience of pain is nonmaterial, but that is not how I would ordinarily think of it. I was trying to hear something like a random conversation nearby and heard, "Drowned people in the brush." Both "drowned" and "brush" seemed to represent the muffled unclear quality of what I was trying to hear. It was unclear, so it clearly says it is unclear! Again, this choice of language and conception was not one normal to me. Another time I was listening and heard, "Anybody over the telephone?" It represented the act of trying to pick up conversation.

More complex examples of this autosymbolic level can be given. It is possible to watch feeling shape itself vaguely and then explode in an image or something said. Sometimes it would be a word or name that had no meaning in itself. Once I heard "Edward Conze," another time "Anzeema." More recently someone asked, "Where is the Ogalala?" My impression is that these names reflect a particular inner state in their sound qualities. For instance, Oga for me has some implication of something big, powerful, and threatening. Lala I associate with pleasant wandering. "Where is the Ogalala?" then has the implication of searching for something powerful in this wandering inner state. The process feels autosymbolic, though with an odd name, "Edward Conze," and sound, "Anzeema," I am on less certain ground. At the moment the name explodes in awareness it seems to represent the background feelings it came from by the arrangement of its sound qualities.

On another level the hypnogogic seems to be instructing the person. At this level one may have enough experience to be able to question the process and have it answer back. Like the rest of the hypnogogic, these dialogues are often brief. One wakes up too much to stay in the process. And the dialogue doesn't always make nice clear sense. It isn't like talking to one's self. It is more like talking to a very playful stranger who thinks symbolically. While meditating on a headache I heard, "There is an old bitch or bastard and you can't see how intimate he is. Concentrate on the pain. It is useful." This sounded like instruction. I was already suspecting that meditating on pain had use, so much of the statement could have been autosymbolic of this. The "old bitch or bastard" was about the way I felt about the pain. The making of an unseen male or female person out of it really surprised me. The lesson to be learned from this was unclear.

Once I asked who was speaking and heard, "A soul in the next place." I asked what next place and heard, "The episode of the pregnant———" It was cut off by my becoming too alert. But "The episode of the pregnant———" didn't sound as though I were going to learn of the next place in any easy fashion! I once asked, "What do you think of my lying in bed?" and immediately heard, "Nut." I asked if it were harmful in someway and my own word "harmful" was turned into "horrible." My question instantaneously became its answer. I have had many indications that the hypnogogic doesn't approve of my staying in bed in the morning on the pretext of studying this state. It has never objected to my losing sleep time at night while studying it. I once asked the hypnogogic whether or not I should change jobs and circumstances. For once I got a nice clear answer. I saw a river that had worn down through a gorge for centuries and heard, "Wear down like a river." I came out of it with a feeling of the great pleasure of knowing one place for centuries. This looked purely instructive. Sometimes the instruction is a bit beyond my understanding. For instance, I was thinking of the meaning of a dream while half awake and heard, "Liberal instruction is Beethoven's paycheck." I can only guess at the meaning of this. Beethoven was a man who gave much to the world by pouring out himself in music. It seemed to say the one who gives liberally of himself will be rewarded by liberal instruction.

Most of my dialogue with the hypnogogic has taught me something of myself and more of the playfully elusive quality of the inner processes. The following is an odd and beautiful example of this. I was about to reject the hypnogogic and wake up when I suddenly heard, "Don't you like my sister?" I quickly inquired, "Who is your sister?" The process answered, "Heaven. Talk to me now." I said, "Tell me of your nature," and got as an answer, "Handsome breath." After such a dialogue you are left with the feeling something nice has transpired but you are not sure what! The words spirit and breath have the same Latin root. Roughly, the above incident seemed to say that by rejecting the hypnogogic I was rejecting the hypnogogic's sister, or heaven. The hypnogogic's own nature is handsome breath, which I take as a noble spirit—whose sister is heaven. This brings us to the deepest level of the hypnogogic.

I prefaced the whole matter of the hypnogogic by saying that it is a difficult state to reach and deal with. Within it, its deepest level is a kind of satori or enlightenment. Suddenly the questioner and the answerer are one. This one breaks into infinite images of all its representations. The individual awakens as though from a trance, puzzled by what was suddenly seen and experienced. On one of these occasions I experienced a gigantic mandala, which is a fourfold symbolic image of the real self.[7] It was an intricately and deeply carved Oriental wood design of a fourfold form. The center of the design was an empty hole through which the fearsome force of the universe whistled.

If the hypnogogic is explored just deeply enough to see feeling form into words and to catch autonomously appearing images and words, the experience begins to modify ordinary daily life. Having caught images and words popping into the head from nowhere, you begin to see them also in daily life. You can better recognize the autonomous given. What you might normally have accepted as your own thought begins to be seen as "out of the blue." You begin to feel much more like an observer of a process rather than the only one ruling your own head. Your own head and experience becomes more like a meeting place of many. The individual becomes a bit more modest about his own processes. It is as though he has begun to experience the rolling hills and distant seas of the psyche and feels much less presumptuous about his own scope. Yet, as the individual sees the inner acting playful and wise, he gains more confidence in beauty and wisdom within. It is a somewhat odd world within, and yet it is a "handsome breath."

Summary

1. Images seen with eyes closed (eigenlichts), the hypnogogic state, and dreams are perhaps on a single continuum.

2. It is difficult to poise between sleeping and waking in the hypnogogic state. Most of the early lessons in this state involve learning to keep one's ego quiet so inner processes can emerge.

3. The great advantage of the hypnogogic state is that ego can observe and even deal with processes that are autonomous and outside its bounds.

4. There may be levels in this state that may relate to one's

own understanding and dealing with the state.

5. A rough hierarchy of levels would seem to be represented by:

(a) random bits of images and phrases;

(b) experiences that are pretty clearly autosymbolic or representative of one's state at that moment;

(c) hypnogogic experiences that are instructive, including the possibility of questioning the process and learning from it;

(d) hypnogogic experiences that break into trancelike periods of enlightenment.

6. Experiences with this state tend to:

(a) make one able to see similar experiences in normal consciousness;

(b) make one less presumptuous of his personal powers and, correspondingly;

(c) make one more confident of beauty and wisdom in the natural depths of mind.

8

Dreams

Throughout the whole night I seemed to be going deep down, by ladders and other spaces, but quite safely and securely, so that the depth did not bring me into any danger, and there occurred to me in the dream the verse, "Lowliness or other things, be they coming or. . . ."

Emanuel Swedenborg, *Journal of Dreams,* April 7–8, 1744

The dream is a relatively complex realm of its own. Whole volumes have been devoted to research on the dream, dream content, and approaches to dream interpretation.[1] It is sufficient here if we grapple with the dream enough to understand what it indicates in our descent into the natural depth of man. Dreams have been explored much more than fantasy, meditation, or the hypnogogic state. Perhaps dreams leave a clearer and more dramatic product than these other states. For example, after awakening from a dream of wrestling with a tiger one is impressed by this dramatic life scene left in one's awareness unbidden.

Almost everyone knows dreams occur and most people have

made at least a minor effort to work out the implications of some of their own dreams. Most of them have seen themselves doing embarrassing or illegal things in dreams, and this may well have contributed to the lack of attention paid to their dreams!

At various times dreams have been used by witch doctors, the religious, and psychotherapists. Actually these apparently disparate groups are on a continuum of efforts to understand inner processes. As religions became less experiential and more dogmatic, they largely abandoned the dream some centuries ago. Psychotherapists went through a flurry of interest in the dream following Freud's classic *Interpretation of Dreams*.[2] Except for a few psychotherapists and psychoanalysts trained in the older school, professional interest has tended to fade too. This fading came, in part, as psychotherapists learned to focus more and more on the present observable behavior of clients. Fritz Perl's remarkable skill with dreams has been something of a revival within Gestalt therapy.[3] In some humorous way the whole history of civilization could be depicted as successive waves of interest in dreams. Each wave would represent a renewed interest in penetrating the woods of the psyche—to be followed by a lessening interest and turning again to external things.

Facts on Dreams

Present-day experts on dreams would include the relatively few psychotherapists who have used them and common people who have learned to read their message. There are some broad facts about dreams that experienced people are inclined to agree upon.

1. The dream is best recalled while still half asleep just after dreaming. It should be written down or dictated into a tape recorder then. Hours or days later one will have lost whole parts of the dream, if it can be recalled at all. A dream needs con-

scious review in order to become memorable. We must make a mental note here that the more inner a process, the more likely it can occur without memory.

2. The real meanings of a dream lie in the unique life experience of the dreamer. Dream-book, cookbook-type interpretations, while entertaining, are not generally valid. It is only because we have somewhat similar life experiences that there is any similarity at all in dream meanings from one person to another.

3. People frequently ask why they don't dream. There is solid evidence that most people have four to five dreams a night! Dreams occur as one goes over the threshold from waking to sleeping and another dream occurs when one comes out of deep sleep, approaching the threshold of waking. The real issue is why people don't remember dreams. They have simply neglected to pay attention to them and the dream process itself isn't disturbed enough to produce nightmares. All kinds of personal efforts to recall dreams can pay off. Keep a pad and pencil by the bed. Talk to yourself about dreaming as you go to sleep. Decide you will even write down dream fragments. Talk with people who are interested in dreams. Some chemicals seem to increase dream recall, but I won't name them because they haven't been tested out sufficiently. Mostly it is simply a matter of trying.

4. Dreams are primarily visual experiences, though they can involve all of the senses. A few people rarely dream visually. One person of my acquaintance had mostly auditory dreams.

5. Color is fairly common in visual dreams. It begins to appear that those who don't note color in dreams are less color conscious.

6. External sounds and sensations can be incorporated into dreams, or more often they are overlooked. When they are incorporated, they are woven into the meanings in the dreamer's life.

98

7. Many people are plagued by repetitive dreams. They may be identical each time or vary somewhat. This is perhaps the simplest of all psychic disorders to deal with. Any real effort to unlock the meaning of the dream will tend to end the repetition. The repetition seems to indicate the dreamer is stuck in a particular reaction.

8. Nightmares are unusually vivid and disturbing dreams. They can occur in illness or fever. Because they are so rich in meaning they are particularly valuable to understand.

9. Dreams appear to be an entirely normal phenomenon. They seem to occur almost from birth in infants. They appear to occur in other animals too.

10. Some people feel they can fashion their own dreams. At best one can inject a few elements into dreams, but one can't structure the whole dream. Events that caught one's attention and then were quickly overlooked during the day are most likely to be dreamed about at night.[4] Under hypnosis one can suggest that a subject dream around a particular problem or event. These dreams, too, are very symbolic, so that it is not immediately apparent how the dreamer got from the given problem to the dream.

11. Dreams are primarily a symbolic or dramatic representation of the present life concerns of the individual. It is not really known why they are so symbolic.

An observation of Eugene Aserinsky in Nathaniel Kleitman's laboratory led to a series of valuable findings on dreams.[5] It was observed that individuals showed random eye movements (REM) when dreaming. When REM showed and they were awakened, they reported dreaming. Awakened without REM, they reported no dreaming. Electroencephalographic tracings (EEGs) also could be used to tell when individuals dreamed. With these tools a number of findings were made. Most individuals dream for about 20 percent of their sleeping time. The dreamer periodically partially arouses from deep sleep, dreams three to sixty minutes, and then falls back into deep dreamless sleep. A man of seventy-five will not only have slept twenty-five years, but he will have spent some five years dreaming! The time taken to dream is roughly comparable to that taken for the same events in life. Infants spend 60 percent of the time dreaming; the percent of dreaming time diminishes through the teens, reaches another low peak in the twenties, and seems to diminish through the rest of life. Persons who have trouble recalling dreams seem to spend less time on each dream.

The most interesting findings came when persons were prohibited from dreaming. Take two groups of normal persons, assiduously awaken one group every time they start to dream and awaken the other group a comparable amount when they aren't dreaming. The two groups will sleep an equal amount but one will be dream-deprived. The dream-deprived group will become emotionally disturbed in three to six days. After six days of this a dream-deprived person will start dreaming almost as soon as his eyes are closed and stubbornly resist awakening. It is clear that the dream has some function in restoring internal balance whether or not it is ever interpreted. To dream is not only natural, but is somehow fundamentally necessary, though we don't really know why. My own guess is that this reflects a homeostatic or balancing within brain processes themselves— and that corresponding to this, on a higher level, the balancing occurs within the psychic meanings in an individual's life. On the psychic level, I suspect that we have to experience meanings, worries, concerns, that we would prefer to keep from awareness. They will be experienced in symbolic form in sleep if nowhere else.

Interpreting the Dream

The primary difficulty in understanding the dream is that it doesn't bother to speak our language. Rather than try to understand the dream from the viewpoint of sober rational consciousness, one should try from the closer, dream state. Note all associations. Even though they don't seem relevant at first, they are one's earliest keys to the meaning of the dream. After one becomes accustomed to the odd language of the dream, it is easier to work out meanings.

One year, near Thanksgiving time, I was offered a temporary appointment at a leading university as a full professor of psychology. Shortly thereafter I dreamed that I had been given a big turkey. I was delighted with it until I pulled off a drumstick and discovered long white lines or worms in the meat. The final feeling of the dream was, "Boy, I'm lucky, but what is this white stuff?" I immediately associated turkey, Thanksgiving, with the offered honor. The white lines stumped me. I was stepping out of a bank later in the day and saw the white line down the street and suddenly saw the meaning. The honor had one flaw, I'd have to do a lot of driving—a lot of white lines. That's what spoiled the turkey gift. Once the dream is understood, all parts of it make sense in terms of one's own experiences.

Unlocking the meaning of the dream requires some real understanding of its nature. It is possible to generate dreams and thereby study their mechanism. This has been done by hypnotizing a subject and then suggesting that he will dream about a particular problem. The dream symbolizes the problem. One has to go back through the individual's life experience and associations to see why such symbolism was chosen. The individual doesn't fashion the dream. Under hypnotic suggestion it simply forms around the suggested issue or problem.

I recently discovered it is possible to do this to yourself. Before you have fully awakened in the morning, think of an issue in your life that concerns you. Hold that issue in mind and you may suddenly walk into a dream. One morning I generated about ten dreams. The main difficulty was that I would forget what I was thinking about and became caught up in the symbolism of the dream. This may be the trouble with dreams too. The innermost person reflects on a concern, a dream forms, and the concern it represents is lost. Finally I wrote down the concern so I wouldn't lose it: "I will reflect on my future." Suddenly I saw a young man sitting high on a cliff, knees drawn up, staring out to sea. He seemed very quiet and meditative. But I was concerned whether the cliff was safe. It seemed to be made of soft sandstone. There were many pockets in it. There were also tough little tufts of beach grass. I was worried whether the whole thing would hold up. His eyes were on the distant sea.

Associations helped penetrate its meaning. Since I was a young man I've dreamed of sailing around the world in a small boat. The young man with eyes fixed on the distant sea seemed to remind me of that. Such a voyage would mean a real chance to reflect on things, as he was doing. It was still somewhat distant, so he was on land looking at the sea. My own worry was whether he was safe. He wasn't worried. I worried that all this would hold up—I had been concerned whether this dream of going around the world would hold up. The tough tufts of grass were more puzzling. To understand them I had to examine the image closely. This spiny grass was many sharp possibilities, holding on tenaciously. Though there were few tufts, they seemed to hold the cliff itself together. I couldn't help but admire the tough tenacity of the grass. The spiny grass reminded me of many choice points each of which was painful. When I looked at the whole evolvement of my dream to sail around the world, it had involved many little painful choice points—but it was tough, tough enough to hold up. I worried unnecessarily. The young man wasn't worried. The cliff looked old; there was no recent earth movement, and the grass held it together. The cliff itself was very tactile, the kind of soft sandstone I would think of carving as the weather has already done. And, indeed, my dream was tactile, malleable, carvable; it could change under the work of my own hands.

This is the real nature of the dream. It reflects some kernel of reflection on one's life. It represents this visually as a scene and events. *Everything in the scene is the dreamer.* The most conscious feelings of the dreamer are his in the dream. Less conscious aspects are represented by others. The more alien the others are (i.e., different in age, race, disposition) the more alien are those aspects of the self. Even the objects in the dream are parts of the self. In the above dream I am the one who is worried if this will all fall down. This is my most conscious aspect. The young man looking out to sea is a little less conscious. He isn't worried. He is more of a future potential. The cliffs and the grass are the actual circumstances of my life, including sharp choice points, tenacity, etc. The ocean, the wide sweep of the sea, is what I look to—what I hope for. Its extensive placid form represents the feelings of a meditating young man. Everything in the dream is fashioned out of the life of the individual and it reflects that life. What he can't recognize in that life looks "other" to him in the dream too. But of course that is how we all live! Neither in the dream nor in life do we recognize all the selves with which we have peopled our environment.

Now that the dream is better understood, there are several further keys to working out its meaning beyond associating to parts of it.

1. Assume everything in the dream is you. If you are puzzled what a part could mean, examine it in fantasy, as I did the tufts of grass.

2. Reverse roles. If you can't see another person in the dream as yourself, mentally reverse roles with him. Enact his role and

tell the stupid dreamer what you are trying to do or get across.

3. Paraphrase the dream and listen in the paraphrase for its meaning. In the above dream I'd say, "Someone is looking peacefully out to sea, but I'm worrying if it will all hold up." I could recognize my "looking out to sea" and my worry about its all holding up.

4. Do most of the work on your dream while half asleep when you can feel back into it and halfway understand the symbolic language of your inner self.

5. Look for embarrassing little comments on yourself in dreams. Most dreams aren't very complimentary. They throw some light on inner attitudes and feelings. At best their compliments are mixed with wry criticism. After I completed my Ph.D. dissertation, which I thought a brilliant contribution to thought, a dream described it as a fairly good painting but done in such drab tones.[6] I must admit it was a bit heavy and somber. In the dream the painting was locked away in a closet. However great the thesis is, it has been locked away for two decades since the dream.

6. Don't look too hard for prediction in dreams. They can be predictive but one seldom knows what is predicting what until the predicted event occurs. Often dreams predict little scenes that seem of no particular importance. A woman dreamed in color of a child's drawing. She even told others of it. Ten years later she saw it as the recently done work of a ten-year-old- girl. But of what importance was this? A large part of the predictive power of a dream comes from its having the same information you do. Most often the dream is speaking of your present. It may reflect your own future fears instead of accurately reflecting the future. While it can predict, this is seldom its aim.

7. In general, the dream reflects your deepest thought. Its wisdom may well transcend your ordinary understanding.

8. There are big dreams. They have much more impact to the dreamer, may be in intense color, feel more impressive,

may awaken the dreamer, and are more easily remembered. Big dreams are likely to reflect a major turning point in one's insight.

The following long dream came from a well-educated Mexican psychology student. We worked on the dream for about an hour before all parts of it became clear.

I am in a beautiful German baroque town with old wooden buildings. We are there because a flood is coming to destroy and cover it. We want to preserve the town somehow, so we are there to photograph it before it goes under water. I have a fine 35mm camera with a huge telescopic lens on it. There are other people there with telescopic lenses. We line the main street waiting for the flood to come. Water begins to come down the main street and we catch it with our cameras. Suddenly the flood turns into a parade. As the soldiers on parade go by they begin to ask random questions. I begin to feel fear. We are now sitting on a bench in a line. We are being interrogated by three Nazi soldiers. One is fifty, rather nice, with wrinkled clothes, not like the Nazi stereotype. Nevertheless he has an iron helmet on. When someone goes to be interrogated we all shift down one seat. They don't come back and I conclude they are being killed.

The older soldier seems friendly so I think to use my forty dollars to bribe him. I ask to talk to him. He seems happy to do so. I say, "I don't know what this is all about, I have nothing to do with this. I don't know anything of politics and I don't care to know all these Americans. I am a Latin-American tourist and have nothing to do with this." He begins a lengthy speech to convince me Hitler is doing great things. I become enraged. "What the hell is the matter with you, you idiot? Don't you read history? Don't you know Hitler is going to die in 1945?" I end my angry speech with, "Hitler is a maniac and a faggot!" He looks deeply hurt and takes his gun from its holster and hands it to me. He helps me point the muzzle of the gun at his heart and pull the trigger. There is no bang, but blood gathers on his shirt. I walk with my arm around him to the other side of the room. He ends another speech praising Hitler with "And we will take over Latin America." I take this to mean that we would see each other there. I feel very righteous and strong as I argue with him by waving the gun in his face. He is leaning against a mirror. There is an odd sensation as I see my wildly gesticulating image in the mirror. Though I feel like a mild person I see a big man with a gun in his hand. I know I am out of danger of dying. The other people's cameras have turned into machine guns and they are rushing around killing Nazis. I go to my wife on the bench. She can read on my face that everything is all right.

The dreamer was a mild-mannered polite man. He associated with baroque one of the loveliest periods in Mexican history—a period of beauty and graceful living. By preserving the baroque German town he indicated he wanted to hold to what was a graceful, artistic way of living. Yet he couldn't keep to it. This loveliness was to be drowned by a flood—marching soldiers, aggressive Nazis—an aggressive take-over. This contrary trend was more unconscious in him. The older soldier reminded him of his father—a stiff-necked bully in the guise of a pleasant old man. The Nazi's helmet reminded him of the curve of his own long hair. As he went over the angry dialogue with the Nazi he caught himself pounding his own hands together. In the dream there is a transformation in which the old soldier-father aids the dreamer to get rid of him. Then he sees himself in the mirror. He himself is waving his gun and acting aggressively. He denies any interest in politics and then stoutly defends Latin-Americans. In the intimate shooting scene and viewing himself in the mirror the dreamer begins to see that he is aggressive and asserting his rights and beliefs. He is no longer the polite, compliant Mexican. As he becomes assertive, everyone does. He's on such intimate terms with his wife that he doesn't need to explain all this to her. She is part of his own understanding.

The main message of the dream was that though he would have liked to preserve his polite way of living, this side of him was being replaced by the strong, almost aggressive man who would stand up against injustice. He hadn't recognized this trend in himself though he was acutely sensitive to it in others. Hence, in the dream, he would rather not face up to it. Maybe he can bribe his way out. Or maybe he can just dissociate himself from these Americans. It's not that easy. The older soldier, father, his own unconscious identity, catches his eye. The inner, more aggressive identity aids him to kill it as something other, but in turn he finally sees himself as an aggressive man with an imperial hatred of imperialism. It's all right to be this way. The others shoot Nazis too. In the end it is said everything will be all right. There is danger as long as this aggressive trend is seen as belonging only to others. In reality, as he came to recognize his own aggressiveness he could better control his own situation. He was no longer a baroque anachronism that can be put upon by others.

The dream implied in several ways that he began to have insight into these new trends appearing in him. This was implied by the Nazi's friendliness, by his becoming angry like him, by his seeing himself in a mirror acting like him, and by his wife's ability to read it all in his face. Until he got past trying to deny this trend (bribing the soldier, denying association with Americans), people were killed one by one. It said his unconscious aggressiveness was more dangerous than the conscious kind—once he got over the change in his own image. The implication of the end of the dream was that he was standing up for his rights. When his own imperial tendencies became conscious, people would be less able to run over him. This was a relatively long and rich dream that illustrated something of the power of the dream when in full flower. It was a big dream. He remembered it easily months afterward, for it had to do with a major shift occurring within him. The shift was not yet complete. It was still coming. It might take months or years to become complete. But the essential meanings of the shift had been commented on by the dream.

One can enjoy dreams much as one might enjoy a painting or the richness of a good play. Some are like little pieces of art. The following dream occurred to me as I was about to set to work on this book.

A number of us are working on clay. I'm in one room and a group is in another room. I seem to be just awakening to the process. We shouldn't lay out too much clay at once or it will harden. The clay is raked by a fork that cuts it into three-quarter-inch square tiles; it is then coated with glaze and fired. There are to be just blue and white tiles because we are making a scene of an ocean wave. I realize that the work will be accomplished. The word abraxas is associated with this work.

To analyze this: "A number of us are working on clay. I'm in one room and a group is in another room." (I am at the beginning of making something—a book. All of us—me are working at it). "I seem to be just awakening to the process." (It only recently occurred to me that I really could do a book.) "We shouldn't lay out too much clay at once or it will harden." (I have trouble with ideas running off in all directions at once. If I lay them all out at once, I seem too abstract or hardened.) "The clay is raked by a fork that cuts it into three-quarter-inch square tiles and then coats them with glaze and fires them." (The dream counsels me that the book process is simple—cut into little squares like pages and each page in itself is relatively simple.) "There are to be just blue and white tiles." (It is simple —blue and white—black and white pages—my boat—the sea?) "Because we are making a scene of an ocean wave." (Two associations—ocean wave a delicate complex picture of life such as this book is intended to be. Also, the book might actually enable me to go to sea.) "I realize that the work will be accomplished." (This is the point of the whole dream. It says I am working with others, that is, have help. The process is simple— by building up many little pieces we can capture an image of life. I am just awakening to this possibility.) "The word abraxas is associated with this work."

This little touch in the dream needs to be explained at length. For a long while I was concerned to be able to tell what stemmed from my own will and what was autonomous or other.

Eventually I was given many signs on which to make this distinction. The word abraxas means nothing to me beyond its sounding Greek. It is a kind of signature on the dream that says, "Signed by the other." When I looked up abraxas, I found that it has a number of lovely implications. It was engraved in Greek on little tiles known as abraxas stones. The practice came from Basilides and his followers, early second-century gnostics who had some contact with St. Peter, but their doctrines have been lost. The Greek letters for abraxas "make up the number 365, and the Basilidians gave the name to the 365 orders of spirit that emanated in succession from the supreme being. These orders were supposed to occupy 365 heavens, each fashioned like but inferior to that above it, the lowest being the abode of the spirits who formed the earth and its inhabitants, to whom was committed the administration of its affairs."[7] The stone could be used for magic, but its main meaning was that the bearer understood how he was an emanation of the supreme being. Of course, I was most honored to have abraxas associated with this work.

I did imply above that one shouldn't always find compliments and great promises in dreams. Buried in the symbolism of the dream are also a few criticisms. It says I worry too much—the book can be done. Unlike my expectations, it will be done in a lot of little pieces. It also says don't take on too much at a time or the work will die (harden). I also suspect that an ocean wave is a bit too lively a thing to capture with simple blue and white tiles, or the psyche with words.

Still it is very comforting to get and understand a message like this. The fact that the source of the message knows more than I do (abraxas) is part of this comforting quality.

Personal Uses of Dreams

The main value of the dream can be obtained when the individual can read back the meanings of his own dream. This is in addition to the value of the dream as part of some kind of natural homeostatic mechanism in the psychic economy. *The only meanings in a dream that you can use are those that you can relate to your own life.* A clever friend may discover your *anima* or soul figure in a dream, but this is of no use to you unless it related to how you live. It may well not even be true. And if true, useless. A Zen monk once called such brilliant formulations flowers in the air (i.e., pretty but unreal). Even if you were mistaken that a dream fragment reflected a particular concern, this is still of value to you. You are more likely to associate a particular worry to part of a dream if it is a real worry to you. And your associating this meaning to part of a dream is more likely an accurate interpretation than almost anyone else's guess. As you become handier in associating meaning with parts of dreams you will get better and better at recognizing a good fit and interpretations that don't fit so well. The real and most useful meanings are the ones that surprise and shock a bit and seem to fit *for you* like hand and glove. I would just add the proviso that there may be more meanings than this. It is possible for a dream to have several levels of meaning simultaneously, i.e., talking about events in several periods in your past, talking about present concerns, reflecting new values, and intimating your probable future—all in one dream. Finding one set of hand-and-glove meanings doesn't exclude others. But above all, those you feel are most likely accurate are the only ones you can use anyway.

There are several possible uses of a personal study of your own dreams:

(a) to remind you of your needs;

(b) to give you another perspective on what you are doing;

(c) to warn when you are getting out of sorts with others;

(d) to give an inside view of the value of significant others in your life;

(e) and to clarify your real values.

Each of these uses can be briefly illustrated. We are quite capable of forgetting our own needs. If we get too far off base the dream will dramatize the need. A common example are sexual needs. It is normal, for instance, for those with no present sexual outlet to approach or reach a climax in dreams. In males this leads to the wet dream with actual emission. We can go beyond the mere discovery of sexual needs by studying exactly how they are portrayed in a dream. For instance, a man who finds himself making love to a particular woman would do well to study this woman *who is also a part of himself.* He might try to amplify her—her characteristics in his mind's eye, i.e., "I am a shy, sensitive girl who waits for the man to make the first move. I'm inclined to be lonely, waiting, hoping." The man has these tendencies in him and needs to meet with, unite with, and accept them. This is a meaning that could lie under a simple sexual need. Other common needs portrayed in dreams are the need to rest, to be alone or with others, to be respected by others, etc. For instance, a person who drives himself too much could have dream in which he is falling down, dying, and this is not noticed by others (himself).

It is possible for an individual to adopt a particular course of action, all nicely explained to himself, only to find that his own dreams put an entirely different meaning on it. In one of my earliest experiences as a member of a psychotherapeutic group, the others in the group came to the consensus that I was holding them at a distance and not really joining in with them. I vigorously defended that I was really with them. That night I dreamed I was examining people with an inverted telescope that made them more remote. The dream was like a slap in the face. It said the same thing the group did. Having been hit by the group and my own dream, I had to admit to myself and the others that they were right. It was then more possible to get closer to them.

People normally vary somewhat in outlook and disposition. One individual may become paranoid for a while, another depressed, etc. Dreams will often be given to reflect that this change is coming. When I'm paranoid in dreams I'm a little extra careful about interpreting the motives of others for a while. In a similar way some primitives would deal with the dream as a reality. If the primitive man had raped a neighbor's wife in a dream he would apologize to her and her husband. Our society is probably not mature enough for such an out-front approach, but at least the dreamer can bear in mind his assaultive tendencies for a day or so.

Dreams will occasionally turn around your view of another person. A kindly gentleman may be portrayed that night as a sinister figure or a gauche friend may suddenly appear as brilliant. I would simply take this bit information as one more possibility regarding the real character of the person. It may or may not be accurate. The kindly gentleman may or may not be sinister. According to the dictum that all parts of a dream are yourself, this sinister gentleman is also one of your own aspects. Yet the dream may use him as a sinister figure because the inner you sees sinister attributes in him. He fits the role.

It is possible to discover your own deepest values in dreams. It is easy to get caught up in the workaday world and overlook inner tendencies that have never really seen the light of day. Dreams will show them over and over again. And don't assume that all inner tendencies must have to do with base sex or violent tendencies. I recall one woman who was taught to put down American Indians as worthless bums, only to be instructed in her dreams to sense the greatest values the Indians had known. She was part Indian, and it was herself that had been put down and was elevated. I recall neurotic women who were terrible mothers and housekeepers being introduced in dreams to the Magna Mater, who enjoyed caring for all. And I've known more than one criminal who found concerns for honesty and service to others in dreams. You may feel you are really a sincere, kind, nice person only to find you are cutting up and burying friends in dreams. Discovery of your own tendencies may lead up or down. The friends you are killing may be both those real people out there and part of yourself. In some respects the dirty dark parts of dreams are more valuable than kind intimations of one's own greatness. We all suspect our greatness, but the dark side is less known.

Summary

The dream is a fully formed message from the other side of individuals. It is valuable because it is so little contaminated by personal wishes. Its greatest difficulty lies in the fact that the other side doesn't bother to speak one's own language (unlike most visitors from outer space on television). It is a personal, delicate, and somewhat difficult process to unlock this foreign tongue. There are a number of possible values in doing so. The central key is that all parts of the dream are you. The dream is fashioned out of your life and speaks your life. The mystery of the dream's choice of symbolic language will be examined later.

* * *

Emanuel Swedenborg's dream that opened this chapter will make more sense after the reader has learned its background. It is from what may be the oldest dream series ever recorded. It come in the period in which Swedenborg was changing from a scientist to a psychologist-mystic. He had mastered all of the sciences of his day and founded several new ones. The fields he had mastered were as diverse as geology, astronomy, and human anatomy. It was also a period in which he was studying dreams and inner states. He was literally going down within. The journey for him was very safe. The verse comes from a religious hymn. He was soon to be introduced into heaven and hell. This was the whole of the recorded dream. He offered no associations to it nor did he interpret it as he has often done with others. I suspect its meaning was apparent to him.

9

The Shape of Madness

Therefore my loins are filled with anguish;
   pangs have seized me,
   like the pangs of a woman in travail;
I am bowed down so that I cannot hear,
   I am dismayed so that I cannot see.
My mind reels, horror has appalled me;
   the twilight I longed for
   has been turned for me into trembling.

"Fallen, fallen is Babylon;
and all the images of her gods
   he has shattered to the ground."
Oh my threshed and winnowed one. . . .
               Isaiah 21:3–10

Of what value is it for the average person to understand mad-ness? In the whole realm of tinkering inside one's head, mad-ness represents the end point of the worst binds one can get into. By its grossness, madness illustrates and underlines beauti-fully stupidity in dealing with one's own resources.

    Several other functions are also served. A common myth and

fear is that delving into the private inner space itself could lead to madness. The natural language and mode of operation of the inner sound remarkably mad to any "practical-minded person." Also, it is of value to the average person to understand better what madness is, how to get into it, and how to get out of it. Rather than being knowledge possessed by a few experts, it should be part of everyone's equipment. Finally, the gross contours of madness will throw another light on what it means to be fully human.

Some may be puzzled by my use of the term madness. For twenty years I've lived and worked with very crazy people. Some sixteen years were spent as a clinical psychologist in a state mental hospital.[1] It is out of a profound respect for the awesome trap of madness that I exercise the privilege of ordinary language.

Years of work in a mental hospital revealed a curious pattern in the use of words for madness which has a relatively precise diagnostic jargon. This one is a paranoid schizophrenic, that one is a psychoneurotic, hysteric type, etc. This impressive language basically categorizes kinds of odd behavior. It has remarkably little to do with predicting prognosis, understanding patients, or treating them. New hospital staff members were quick to see the impressiveness of this technical language. They learned it and, timorously at first, learned to use it. Lower levels of hospital staff who never really learned the language felt somehow inferior. But the older and more experienced staff tended to drop the language. The mental hospital became a nut house. Some people weren't psychotic, they were crazy. The technical language was reserved for formal occasions when communicating with outsiders. Those who lapsed into plain English were closer to the patients than those who still sounded very professional. Patients could relax and feel more comfortable with the staff member who asked simply, "What got you into this nut house?"

The technical language sounds so profound, yet it merely gives a fancy name to common kinds of human reactions. It treats people as odd objects. It is pretentious and estranging from the real situation. Are we not all mad, that is, human in funny and surprising ways? Madness is common. We all have it and can understand it.

Dr. Paul Frey, a brilliant psychiatrist, carried out this de-mythologizing of mental illness in very practical ways. He was in charge of the units in a mental hospital that housed the most hopeless patients. His patients had often failed a number of gentle, thoughtful, professional psychotherapeutic approaches. He would greet a newcomer with, "Who did you scare to get yourself put in this nut house?" Actually, most people are hospitalized around incidents in which they frightened loved ones. Dr. Frey was giving the person back his feeling of power. The patient could and did scare someone. If he could understand how he scared others and correct that bit of behavior, he could leave the hospital. The usual approach of mouthing mental health euphemisms left the patient in a hopeless bind. "When you are feeling better we can take you to a mental conference and let you go" merely signals to the distraught patient the truth that he is caught in some incomprehensible maze and may have to wait for fate to work it out. "Who did you scare" strikes at the nitty-gritty of madness. It says madness is not some vague mysterious disease of the mind; it has to do with stupidities in human behavior that all are capable of.

One social worker wanted to help a woman who was deeply bothered over all the dead bodies she found under other people's porches. If this woman would only shut up about the dead bodies she could go outside. All her other behavior seemed respectable enough. The social worker counseled the woman to study strangers' reactions when she sprang on them the news of dead bodies. The woman did learn to keep the bodies to herself and was successfully placed outside the hospital.

There are two fundamental ways of getting taken out of life's game. One can violate the laws generated by society and be imprisoned. Or one can simply act in odd ways and be incarcerated as mentally ill. Mental illness is one state code is defined as "requiring supervision, care, or restraint for the welfare of others or the protection of themselves." It says the person bothers others or can't take care of himself. Mental illness is simply the gross end of a whole continuum of conditions that make one fit poorly into society. The neurotic housewife plagues her children and husband and is seen as a little odd by friends. A businessman can be dependent on alcohol and yet not require "supervision, care, or restraint" until he gets falling-down drunk. Whatever madness is, it certainly represents a whole range of conditions, from a mild being out of sorts with others to requring supervision, etc.

Also, it is not a simple matter that can be laid to one cause. Clearly heredity can play a role, as in Huntington's chorea. Some conditions such as mental retardation, certain ones among the aged, and possibly even some schizophrenia involve physical disorders. The mentally retarded, for one reason or another, have a brain that is poorer than most. Some conditions appear to be very much learned, or socially derived. This includes most character disorders, neuroses, and many psychoses. The individual learned a poor mode of adaptation in the company of others. To add to the complexity, it is entirely possible that real madness can be a mix of a hereditary potential affecting body chemistry that affects a person's reactions to others and their reaction to him, which affects his whole social history. We would prefer causality to be simple, single, and linear, but it may well not be.

We can also add another significant dimension to the whole picture as elaborated well by Thomas Szasz.[2] Part of so-called mental illness depends not on what the individual "has" but how others react to him. When we placed crazy people in the community we came to know of towns and neighborhoods in large cities where people simply reacted less to someone who hallucinated out loud or talked to trees. We could place very crazy people out on a small pension in certain parts of town where odd behavior was widely accepted. We had special pre-leave training programs where long-hospitalized patients learned to dress normally (i.e., inconspicuously), to eat with acceptable manners, to operate a telephone, and to shop in a store. Our craziest patients required quite a bit of follow-up social work that mostly involved dealing with the anxieties of those around the patient. A very crazy person could stay out among people who understood and accepted his eccentricities, since part of madness involves what others overreact to. This is the "welfare of others" in the above definition of mental illness. In some societies it is normal to feel that others are trying to poison one's food. In our society these people are paranoid. How much of madness is just the overreaction of others we can hardly say, since we've seldom examined madness in this light. Certainly some of it is. Some schizophrenics would tend to be seen as odd in any society and would not survive in some. We are mostly in the dark about real causality in the realm of madness.

In spite of the complexity of the varied domain of madness I've long asked myself how these people are different. I think it is possible to describe the real hallmarks of madness.

The Hallmarks of Madness

Madness is a turning in on one's self that makes one a constricted uselessness that misses one's highest potentials. Rather than discuss this as an abstract definition I would prefer to illustrate it phenomenologically by what I have seen of madness. Most of my cases come from the grosser end of the continuum, hospitalized madmen, but this does not exonerate the so-called normals. The gross end simply serves to illustrate trends that can be seen in any normal person.

To enter the real domain of madness I once took the drug LSD on the back ward of a mental hospital for a day. I had already had considerable experience with the drug and knew that it amplified my feelings and perceptions. It didn't make me feel crazy, but under it I could see and understand better what was around me. I donned typical patients' clothes while loaded on acid and went on a one-hundred bed chronic ward. This all-male unit was the backwater collection of the chronic mentally ill. Though a few were in their early twenties, most of the men were forty, fifty, or sixty and had long histories of hospitalization. We were locked in an immense day hall of one hundred men, one hundred chairs, and an television rumbling on in the background. Many watched television but barely reacted to it. Those who watched it continued to do so when all of the institutions' televisions went off for three days. I took a chair near the windows where I could see the whole hall of men. At first I looked to see if anyone around me knew I was a doctor of psychology, staff, or at least a new face come to sit among them. There was no sign of recognition. This was pleasant for me. I could relax and become like them, another anonymous face. In the first hour no one spoke to me except one fellow patient who asked me for a match. When I said I had none that ended our relationship. Later the staff, who seemed like white-coated strangers even to me by then, got us all up to march around the day hall. At first I objected to being roused from my seat. Then I learned how to handle it as a patient. I had to go through the motions asked of me, but without really being in it. As I ambled around with the others, I could go on enjoying my own thoughts. Though they could command my body, they couldn't touch me! Later we were sent out into a fenced-in yard for sunning. Given more space, we simply scattered further and went on doing our own thing.

As I felt my way into this society, it became most pleasant. There was a common agreement among us patients that we would not intrude on each others' lives. This included not looking into each others' eyes. If I looked at another's eyes I would intrude in his world and disturb it. I didn't look at them. They didn't look at me. We didn't talk to each other. In fact we left each other really alone.

Then there were some hard lessons to be learned in this alone world. There was neither past nor future, neither inside nor outside. If I were plagued with the past, I would ruminate on what I should have done, could have done, etc. It would be painful to do that for years. Similarly, to think of the future or about getting out would be painful. If I talked to the white-coated strangers they would just politely put me off and I would still be in the alone world. Past, future, getting out were just hang-ups. They burned up in the alone world. What then? Sit and enjoy the bubbling of things in the mind. It was like a slow, aimless masturbation. Nothing big, but so alone there was nothing to compare it to. In this hands-off, left-alone world I was immensely free to do as I wanted. It was like a dimly lit paradise. Though one hundred souls were locked in a single room we were as free as birds. Over there one would be playing with his fingers in his ear like some naughty game. No one noticed. No one cared. There a young man would rise halfway off his seat as though greeting an angel. He was alone. There an old man would be grumbling angrily at himself. He was in a lonely battle. The grumble would come over and over again like a stuck record. There was no one there! I could fart, belch, stare up at the ceiling, do as I pleased (so long as I didn't intrude on others). I was free to diddle; and diddle with diddling; and diddle diddles diddling.

This is a good picture of madness's end point. The mind slips out of gear and no one is around to care about its output. The machine clanks and bangs in its habitual way. There are no stresses, no should/oughts, no hope, no fear. Such a machine would not react if you pointed a loaded gun at its head. Gun. Bang, bang, what's the difference? In the shorthand of the hospital staff these people were called sitters. That was their life's occupation, sitting. It was unpleasant to leave this happy company at the end of the day. I also felt somewhat shaken. I had always felt sorry for sitters, and now I felt sorrier for the staff and myself. I would have to go back again to a world of endless worries. Who would even believe in this odd, dimly lit paradise found by our lowest order of beings, the sitters? I have often thought hippie dropouts could well study under these master gurus of the total dropout.

A number of other observations will further underline the nature of madness, even in its lesser degrees. *Mad people are relatively useless both to themselves and to others.* These two forms of uselessness are essentially the same thing. Those who are useless to themselves are usually useless to others and vice versa. We had all kinds of programs trying to get mad ones back into the work thing. Make work brief, fun, intriguing, financially rewarding, etc., and they would barely limp along. Financial rewards looked the most promising, even when our reward had to be two dollars a month! For the most part mad people can't produce. They have poor work habits, are easily distracted, sense too little of the external situation. In a state hospital the output of well-motivated patients was about one-fourth that of normals. They learned slowly, couldn't retain what they'd learned, and were unusually variable. One college-educated young man had the job of tacking covers on seats. He had a dreadful time deciding where to place the tacks. Occasionally there would be an old woman who had a thing about raking up leaves. She might wear through rakes as fast at they could be supplied. But this was an exception. She wasn't really working or improving the environment in any ordinary sense. She was wiping out the devil's hiding place. Often when I'd be introduced to some normal tradesman as a psychologist he would joke about whether I thought he was crazy. My only reply was, "You can work and produce, you can't be crazy!" Alcoholics are something of an exception. They talk a marvelous game of work, and can even produce briefly. Whenever the staff were given the choice of a really crazy, "burned-out schiz" or an alcoholic, they often preferred the schizophrenic. He would produce less per day, but would in time outdistance the verbally impressive alcoholic.

Madmen turn in on themselves in a variety of ways. One common way is to get locked into their own symptoms. Everyone has talked to the hypochondriac who likes to give everyone a detailed tour of all his physical symptoms. He is even willing to repeat the tour with minor variations day after day. The depressed get locked into their own mood. They can barely perceive or interact with others. Their own mood pulls them in like a gigantic magnet. Psychotics, the real madmen, often bottle up their concerns in some story they want others to join in. Joe K. was trying to get the world to kill off the gangsters that had rotted his brain and homosexualized boys. Many are victims of a gigantic misunderstanding or plot. If only the world would see the light and acknowledge its error. Criminals have just had a few bum breaks and misunderstandings. Neurotics nurse hurts over loved ones. If only others would change. They are sensitive about themselves, easily feel slighted, and easily become defensive. For the most part they see and understand others in unrealistically ideal or evil ways and overlook obvious characteristics. They really misunderstand others. They are rarely able to help others. Even when they fall in love and very much wish to help someone else, they often help the illusory loved one they see and not the real person.

The life space of madmen is constricted. For the sitter the life space might not include even the chair he sits on. His is a life space of irregular illusions. For the hypochondriac the life space might not extend much beyond his own bowels. Contrast this with the gifted normal's life space that includes complex inner events, family, occupation, friends, a hobby, involvment with service clubs, and a careful following of events overseas.

Madmen have, to one degree or another, a lessened ability to care for themselves. Some survive by dint of a limited, routine, undemanding job. Many, even with inherited resources, are still unable to care for themselves. In the state hospital we had to encourage some of them to buy simple necessities such as a belt to hold their pants up.

It is not simple to answer whether mad ones are happy or unhappy. Some observers may feel the hypochondriac enjoys the love affair with bowels. This is doubtful. People who are going into deep madness seem to go through repeated periods of great unhappiness and distress before they get beyond feelings, as in the case of the sitters. One can't really say the sitters are happy—there is too little of a person present to make a judgment of happiness. For the sitter to come back to normality he would have to go through a long period of learning to experience and deal with normal stresses. It seems too long and painful a way back for them. Despite the overwhelming speed and gaiety of the manic, he seems to be skating over a thin ice covering great sadness. For the most part madness and unhappiness are much the same thing. Happiness seems much more a matter of a full living out of one's potentiality even when that living out involves great variation in levels of satisfaction. Certainly the wider life space of normal persons means they live and experience in a wider sphere which is a part of happiness.

A rough sequence of events can be described from normality into deep madness. Little madness is simply a falling out with others. Others don't understand or the world is too harsh. This

124

little madness may come and go as some repeated difficulty with others. In this madness things don't feel the same. Hope becomes less hopeful. The future looks gloomy or uncertain. Existence has a bad taste. One dreams of some miraculous respite. This is normal upsetness.

The madness deepens as one turns away from others in on one's self. The size of the world constricts. Corresponding to this one sees formerly loved ones turn away and become strangers. All the customary hopes and plans fall dead. The individual finds some face-saving explanation. "If only my parents (boss, society, etc.) had been different. If only I had had some breaks." The saving explanation falls on one's health, fate, or, the best of all, on the faults of others. The life space becomes like a mean little cage whose every nook and cranny is painful and boring.

This rather common level of extrangement from one's self and others really deepens when the individual finds too-far-out an explanation. The person may become the anointed of God or there is really a sinister plot afoot—why? Because one is so great and important! The shared world of pleasant social experiences has fallen dead. Parts of the self fail, decay, and become like alien machines that clank noisily in one's head. The beleaguered self shrinks into a frightened mouse about to be crushed in the jaws of nameless fate. In technical terms this is the acute psychotic state. It is perhaps the most painful of all human experiences. Imagine your mind flooded with pictures, words, feelings, ideas, coming and going rapidly with no control. The inner and outer world is torn apart by unbidden feelings and experiences.[3] The individual finally looks mad to everyone.

With the support of a pleasant steady environment and considerate strangers the individual can be guided, limping and partially disabled, back to shared reality. With repeated failure and pain, or simply because he becomes enamored by his own face-saving solutions, some slip deeper into madness. It takes several years to have the mind finally slip out of gear, and it endlessly diddles with its diddles like a useless giant, weird tinker-toy sculpture. Wheels turn, levers clink, and nothing really happens at all. The individual is a sitter, far beyond life's stresses. Many of these patients can tell you in detail how they died and were buried. This is no fantasy. It is quite true. The people that were known by parents and earlier friends are now quite dead. The real world they had known constricted to nothing and there blossomed the phantasmagoria of the mind out of gear, clinking away like a weird sculpture. Sitters do not come back. At best they can be taught to act inconspicuously and live their constricted odd lives on a pension in some tolerant neighborhood. At worst they are fed and kept alive on the back wards of a mental hospital.

The whole path into madness has not a single aspect that everyone hasn't experienced in some degree.

Psychoneurosis. It is better to bottle up individual potential than it is to face and work out the sticky and dubious possiblies in the inner life.

Psychosomatic disorders. The way of living is not correct for the person and the body says so.

Character disorders. The smart guy cuts a few corners here and there, cheats a little. Everyone does it. There isn't any karma or real justice.

Alcoholism. The alcoholic doesn't have a drinking problem. It's the wife, boss, bad breaks, etc.

Drug Dependency. Try far-out, groovy, exciting drug experiences. Worry about the future price to pay is a foolish hang-up.

Paranoid behavior. It is really satisfying to find how others are the real cause of all one's problems.

Psychosis. It is the giant, unique, face-saving insight into the real reality that no one else experiences.

Depression. It is better to fall into a dark mood rather than meet and solve the problems it represents.

Delusions. It is nice to discover important theories that reveal our greatness and perceptiveness.

The Myths of Madness

"People suddenly go stark raving mad." No. Rarely and only with some acute toxic poisoning or brain change does this happen. People go mad slowly, very slowly. They take a whole lifetime over it. Madness shows all kinds of little warnings of itself to people who have any capacity at all to observe others. The pitiful truth is that mad people generally have a whole life of limitation, failure, and retreat.

"Madness leads to dangerous violence." Again this is rare. In twenty years of keeping company with crazy people, some of whom had committed murder, I had only two women scold me enough to make me nervous and one young man warn me off by flashing a fountain pen at me. Mad people do foolish or strange things. They are generally more constricted and less violent then normal people.

"Too much introspection leads to madness." This idea is fostered by extroverted people who find little use or sense in inner processes. Madness may thrust inner experiences and insights at a person because he has failed at even the most limited introspection. As will be seen in the next section, real introspection or self-reflection serves better to prevent madness than it does to cure it.

"Too much religion (sex, or anything else) leads to madness." It is true that some people show a remarkable preoccupation with religion in madness. Often they entered religion late and desperately as a last straw against the forces of madness. It is a symptom more than a cause. In contrast are the millions of people with a lifetime of normal religious experience who don't go mad. It is usually the nonreligious who are entertained by the idea that religion causes madness. At its best religion can prevent or treat madness. A similar situation applies to sexual frustration or excess. The sexual life is an image of the individual's social life. As his relationships with others get messed up, so does his sex life. Really crazy people are generally less sexual than normals.

"Too much insight can produce madness." The implication of this myth is that there are possible deep insights within ourselves that could rock the mind off its foundation. The thought is intriguing enough to make one want to search for such insights! As we shall see, mystical insight tends to knock out ego awareness but this simply makes the person eminently more sane.

The Way Out of Madness

Suppose you awoke one day to find that you had justifiably been hospitalized as mentally ill. To make it worse you are on a back ward with the worst cases. You recall having been emotionally upset for some while, but you feel as though you had been caught in a maze of misunderstandings. Though you feel shaky and unsure of yourself, you don't feel crazy enough to be locked up among so many weird people. When you approach the staff you find you can't simply convince them you are all right now. They look at your chart and refer to specific episodes, some of which you can remember. Your own inner emotional uncertainty is worsened by the weird people around you and the kindly but negative attitude of the staff who feel you should be there. How can you get out?

Self-analysis and insight is not the method of choice. The combination of emotional upset and the reminders of one's failure by the presence of other patients could lead to a protracted and painful self-examination. Even if you were perfectly normal twenty-four hours before and had been hypnotized and put into the hospital, the feeling that you were possibly mentally ill could generate memories of numerous failures and faults. Unknown to most people, the memory tends to reflect the present situation of a person as well as it does the past. When you feel depressed the memory is clouded with depressed recollections. Only when you feel quite good can you recall your successes in a convincing way.

Self-analysis, as described in the previous chapters, is really for the individual who is fairly well off emotionally and has the interest and time to improve his condition. *Self-analysis can prevent mental disorder. It is useful in improving feelings toward one's self and in increasing one's capacities.* When one is caught in a real emotional bind it is of less use, and the deeper the bind, the less use it is.

Instead of sitting and brooding on your fate on this back ward (thereby suggesting to the staff they are correct), there is a clear and straight way out of the bind. It is so simple and obvious that few think of it. Madness is a turning in on one's self and becoming useless. No matter how disabled a person is he should be able to return to routine work. In a hospital this would mean offering to sweep the floor, clean the bathroom, make beds, clean ashtrays, etc.—whatever simple tasks were at hand. It would be well to concentrate fully on the task, so that you swept the best floors of your life. This takes the mind away from preoccupation with its failures and focuses it outwardly. It should be possible to lose awareness of the self at least for brief periods of time. The simple success of the task suggests to the individual that he can be of use. The seeking out of any kind of useful labor and doing it well would make you stand out from the background of anonymous lost souls on the ward, since madness and uselessness are synonymous. The staff would come to assign more complex and responsible tasks.

The next rung up the ladder would come in the quality of

your relationships to others. Be polite and considerate to others even though they are impossible madmen or very irritable staff. Behave as thoughtfully as possible. Study the gestures and behavior of the others. What name do they prefer to be called by —first name or Mr.————? Joke with them where joking is socially appropriate. Be nice to have around and obviously perceptive of and considerate of others. If you did these things, you would not remain long in the hospital. It might take weeks or months, depending on how slow the official wheels turned. Patience is needed; hence the word patient. If you are being considerate of others, you are forgetting yourself for their sake and getting away from a painful brooding on failures. If in willingly seeking useful work you are made to stand out, then your being thoughtful and considerate of others will really make you outstanding. This would be sufficient to get you out.

A few other ways help too. Indicate to the most influential members of the staff that you feel ready to leave, but don't become a nuisance by repeated demands. Be ready with reasonable leave plans that show good use of resources (money, relatives, job, place to go to, etc.). Try to be aware that your psychiatric history has caused the staff to have reservations. In the core of your history is some incidnet that led to hospitalization (you were thought to be suicidal, threatened others, molested children, something). The staff members worry about their responsiblity in returning an individual to the community. It is as though their reputation is on the line when you go out. Whether or not it is true, you need to overcome their worry over the presenting incident. It would then be easier for them to release you. To understand how others see you, and to act wisely in those terms, helps greatly in solving the mystery of madness.

Should you want the care and shelter of a mental hospital, the best way to get in is to dream up bizarre but unthreatening ideas. You can later laugh at thses ideas and get out. It is becoming increasingly difficult to get hospitalization. Simple insanity may not be enough. If worse come to worst one can always profess a few weird ideas and then sit like a catatonic in a public place. Sit frozen. Do nothing. This eventually worries everyone and leads to hospitalization. Also one can improve suddenly and easily. In some twenty years I've known only three people who may have sought a mental hospital for board and room. Two were of borderline sanity. One was a black man who solved the matter of uncomfortable poverty by looking up in the sky and talking to creatures whenever he needed to. More than 99 percent of the people in hospitals really do need some kind of "supervision, care, or restraint for the protection of themselves or the welfare of others." The idea that relatives railroad people into hospitals to get rid of them is mostly a myth. Often, though, the staff feel much better about the sanity of a patient after they see his crazy relatives who come to visit him. It is common that a patient becomes sicker around relatives, for after all the madness developed with them in the first place. Hospital staffs may well choose to regulate, for the welfare of the patient, the dose of relatives that a patient receives.

In madness the self has foundered in dealing with itself. Mad people have a long history of shallow insight. The descent into depth is the capable mind's discovery of its own resources and its underlying foundation. Madness, the pinched-in limited self, means one has foundered in his own understanding. To dip into the miraculous symbolism of the mind may be just more of this foundering. The way out is straight toward the simplest reality. Wash the dishes, sweep the floor. If you are able, perceive others. If able enough, help others. Then, when the pain of the mind foundering in its own resources is past, consider using some leisure in discovering how you tick. But let self-discovery be added to a basic life of useful work and consideration of others. To drop useful work and consideration of others to devote one's self to self-discovery would be to walk dangerously close to madness. Some young people make this mistake; they are painful bores when they start telling of their fantastic dreams and visions just before they ask for a handout. They smoke pot or drop acid for the "fantastic insight gained" and walk straight toward uselessness to themselves and others. They don't notice that their life space gradually constricts down to a dubious love affair with a drug. As their sphere of usefulness constricts, the inner mind signals alarms by the fantastic signals it put out. But they are less and less able to make any use of these signals. The brilliant internal signal machine turns on, but there is no sensible operator around. The man whose vision interests me is the man who can and does lay fine brick walls. His signal machine has an intelligent operator.

Usefulness is the root of the whole matter of madness.[4] The person who is useful to himself is useful to others. Those who are useless to others are useless to themselves. They just exist. There are sitters on back wards spilling out of their heads beautiful visions, bits of ancient myths, and profound insights into reality—all wasted. They often don't have enough social sense even to be able to communicate these adequately to others. Most sitters are relatively mute. In a fundamental way greatness does not lie in the impressiveness of the visions that pour out of the head. The issue is how they are translated into action. In a very human sense the child that has some insight into how she feels about a sibling while playing with dolls, and translates this into some understanding between herself and the sibling, is doing something far greater than the madman who has ancient symbols rattling around in his head. Usefulness and acting constructively toward others is therefore the way out of madness. Hence those who can fall all the way into deep madness have a whole history of relative uselessness. They had never done much. Conversely those who have done a great deal have a low capacity for really getting into madness and staying any length of time. They simply can't make it. They have known the pleasure of feeling useful.

I really believe that the mental health professions have been beguiled by the symbol-making capacity of the mind. The professionals have felt that if they could rearrange the inner mind of crazy people they would become sane. In a mental hospital we had a dreadful time trying to get mental health experts to see the usefulness of simple work. They felt we might just be using patients as slaves. Or work was useful just to tire the body and pass the time. It was easier for the physician to give the patient a pill to put him to sleep. If only we could learn the secret of how to rearrange the inner mind! Rearrange it from outside reality! When work is seen as a profound treatment approach by the staff, its importance can be conveyed to the patient. As the patient begins to feel socially useful again through successful work, the inner processes will change correspondingly. The inner has been rearranged from the outside. *The inner is, after all, a symbolic commentary on the relationship of the person to the world.* As the relationship to the world is worked out, the giftedness of the inside commentary becomes more apparent. These are not separate spheres. One is a symbolic image of the other. As we grab hold of and improve what a person is really doing, the inner improves. The reality of the inner is in what a person does.

The beauty of work is that it can be given in so many sizes, shapes, and doses. A senile, bedridden old woman might like to stuff rag dolls for children, especially if she can see the joy of the children who receive them. A crippled old man in a wheelchair might like to fold towels, fix toys, or sweep a corner of a room —especially if he was respected by those around him for carrying out this responsibility. It is not simply the work itself which is the root, but its meaning in the whole social context. Very psychotic adolescents, who were totally fed up with people, could respond nicely to the care of farm animals. Effeminate and inadequate boys could change radically in a few months of farm work under a very patient and masculine farmer. A boy's adequacy is not in the rearrangement of his internal psyche, but in learning the pleasure of digging trenches in the ground.

Years of experimentation led us to the conclusion that the most effective residential care involved the shaping of the total living environment as a therapeutic community.[5] The patient came into a functioning community in which he was expected by other patients to take on responsibilities. As he did so, his freedoms and rewards increased until he was ready to leave the hospital. It was fantastic to see the way patients could bring about socially acceptable behavior in their peers. This kind of approach has been the most effective treatment of hard-core drug addiction.[6] The therapy is twenty-four hours a day, patient-designed and patient-executed. The staff functions in a background supportive way. But one almost has to participate in such a living community to realize the power in this approach. I have seen an effective patient community make a fairly reasonable man out a wild maniac in about thirty minutes of peer pressure. But these programs are difficult to get started, for they are contrary to tradition in the mental health field.

Summary

Madness is:

A missing of one's own potentials and natural tendencies. There corresponds to this a blossoming of alarm signals from the inner processes.

A turning away from the self and correspondingly the shared world of people.

A painful failure or series of failures with one's self and with others.

A constriction in the scope of one's world and the meaning of one's existence.

A move toward uselessness and unproductivity both in the sense of caring for one's self and for others.

The way out of madness is:

To do useful things to contribute to the environment.

To act with as much consideration and understanding of others as possible.

In both of these one can forget the painful self, at least for a while, and reestablish the self as a meaningful part of the world.

Corresponding to this the relationship to inner feelings and symbols will improve.

Delving into the psyche is helpful only insofar as it is translated into some kind of socially active result.

It is perhaps an odd paradox, but madness is uselessness. Sanity is usefulness. The internal is messed up only insofar as the external is messed up. Mysteriously, the reality of the internal is the external.

10

Hallucinations

When spirits begin to speak with man, he must beware lest he believe them in anything; for they say almost anything; things are fabricated by them, and they lie; for if they were permitted to relate what heaven is, and how things are in the heavens, they would tell so many lies, and indeed with solemn affirmation, that man would be astonished; wherefore, when spirits were speaking, I was not permitted to have faith in the things they related.

Emanuel Swedenborg, *Spiritual Diary* (¶ 1622), 1748

I was talking with a young woman who was distressed over her love affair with an unseen lover. He said the most promising things and claimed great powers. She was found going out the hospital gate, arguing out loud that she didn't want to leave. My task was to be a counselor between her and a hallucinated lover. He was present. At least she could see him. Finally, just for the heck of it, I started talking to him. I asked her to report faithfully what he said and did. It worked. By this simple expedient a way was found to get inside the patient's experiences of hallucinations, and a fascinating story unfolded. Later I was even able to give psychological tests to the patient and his hallucinations as though they were separate people. To my surprise most hallucinations looked much sicker than the patient on the Rorschach Inkblot Test. What was revealed of hallucinations looked remarkably like ancient accounts of spirit possession. My colleagues were generally skeptical about the whole matter, so I described these findings in essentially religious journals.[1]

The basic procedure was simple. I established a simple contact with the person who hallucinated. I simply wished to learn of his experiences. I would not judge him by what his voices or visions said or did. I would speak directly to the "others" and ask questions. The patient would report back word for word what was said, or what they did. I could record both the question and the answer. The procedure needs to be made clear because when I tell people of it some invariably conclude I am talking of my own hallucinations. My own hallucinations are faint ones in the hypnogogic state that don't compare to the patient's.

Before I get into what was found, several common misconceptions should be laid aside. A hallucination is a clear sensory experience of things others cannot experience. The hallucinated person sees, hears, or feels something others around him simply cannot experience. To have hallucinations does not necessarily mean the person is crazy. A common, normal hallucination is to hear one's name called when there is no one around. A person may be visited by a loved one recently deceased. This is so common it should be considered normal. The meeting is often quite brief, it implies great love between the persons, and it seals the relationship in a pleasant way. Also, some religions encourage their members to expect hallucinated experiences, and of course they occur. By themselves these just mean the person is really participating in the religion. A hallucination can be normal.

Hallucinations should be contrasted with illusions. Illusions are misinterpretations and distortions of real sensory experiences. When you are guilty, the wind in the trees may seem to be saying something of your guilt. Once I came into my shipboard cabin at night to find a brilliant plate lying on my bunk. My hair stood on end because it looked otherworldly. Timidly I approached it to find it was a pool of bright moonlight coming through the round porthole. It was an illusion. A delusion is a fixed set of ideas that don't fit with reality. It is related to being deluded, or mistaken. A vision is a revelation given by something seen. A vision is a visual hallucination with a revelation component.

There was little time to explore the patient's hallucinations, even though it was one of the most fascinating of my experiences as a psychologist. My aim was to describe phenomenologically the hallucinated experiences of the patient as accurately as possible. Because the people seen and heard by the patient are almost invariably real to him, I speak of them as though they were real. It appeared a large proportion of our patients hallucinated regularly. The staff put these down as crazy or unreal, so the patients learned to keep quiet about them. I discovered how to tell a good deal about a patient's hallucinations from his gestures. For instance, his eyes would momentarily flash to the left in response to voices while talking with me. I would tell a patient I didn't know something of my guesses of what he was experiencing. This, as well as my accepting the voices as real to the patient and my not judging the patient by his hallucinations, helped me to learn more than the others. A woman, for instance, could have voices suggesting such dirty things that she was afraid she would be judged by this content. I made it clear that I respected her morality as separate from "theirs."

I also learned the voices were afraid of me. They knew I was a psychologist and were afraid I would kill them. It took some diplomacy to strike up a relationship with someone else's voices. Some hallucinations never did get courage enough to talk in my presence, or they would threaten the patient if he repeated what they said.

The patients received no reward for cooperating. Several said they were glad to do it in hopes I might figure out something that could rid them of the voices. I wasn't in charge of releasing them from the hospital, so there was no gain in it for them. I am personally convinced I received a relatively accurate picture except where the voices themselves demanded some holding back. One advantage of my method was that I was given hallucinations word for word as they formed. Moreover, I could ask the hallucinations specific questions. At best patients report old hallucinations to the staff, which, like old dreams, have much missing. Most of these patients are simple people in grave distress. Two factors suggest accuracy. There is much more similarity than difference between each patient's reports. Also, I had opportunities to speak on hallucinations to mixed audiences of staff and patients and was very pleased to have patients I didn't know come up afterward and say I had described their experiences too.

A great variety of hospitalized people hallucinated. Some were new, acute schizophrenics. Some were long-hospitalized schizophrenics. Others were alcoholic, brain-damaged, or senile. Hallucinations are not just the prerogative of one diagnostic group. There were remarkably few signs of diagnostic differences in hallucinations, so they are described as a single group.

The first basic thing I learned is that hallucinations are experienced as fully real. Voices are heard as average volume or even louder than average. I had worked with one woman off and on for four years before I learned that she saw President Gamal Abdel Nasser. She treated Nasser with the great respect due to a president. He sat in am empty chair in my office. When I passed my hand behind him down the back of the chair, she could not see the part of my hand that was behind him. One

alcoholic became mad at the hallucinations that were tormenting him. This fighting man with a long prison record was mad
enough to try to clobber them. He told me of his frustration at
seeing one hospital staff member exactly duplicated on the
other side of the room. He knew one was a fake, but he couldn't
tell which one. On another occasion he was awakened by mili-
tary officers to do some service for his country. As he sleepily
got up and dressed, he noticed something odd about their in-
signia. He knew they were the tormentors and struck out, hit-
ting a wall. The ward staff were surprised at his hand injury the
next day. Voices sound like real voices, not like the faint speech
normals hear as they think. After enough experience with hallucinations the patient may be able to recognize voices from the
other world as against voices from this one simply because they
become familiar with the persons in the other world. Hallucinations can produce real pain that is indistinguishable from normal pain. The only difference is that voices often will threaten
pain just before it is felt.

In no case did patients accept the term hallucinations for
these experiences. The term was offensive. It implied they were
not real. Almost all patients had private terms of their own for
these experiences: The Other Order, The Eavesdroppers, etc.
A hallucination called "An Emanation of the Feminine Aspect
of the Divine" suggested the terms higher order and lower
order to me to distinguish fundamentally different classes in the
world of hallucinations, and I will later use these terms.

Most patients reported that the other world introduced itself
suddenly to them. One man was riding a bus and he heard a
piercing scream. He pleaded for it to come down in volume,
and it did. One woman was just working in her garden and a
kindly man started talking to her when no one was around. One
alcoholic heard voices coming up a hotel light well. When he
listened he heard them plotting his death. Another man saw a
spaceship land and green men getting out. It takes a while for

the patient to figure out that he is having private experiences that are consequently not shared by others. Often they tell their friends only to find that their sanity is doubted. They therefore learn early to keep quiet about these things. There may be one or several figures. Some familiar ones come around day after day, such as one an old codger called "The Old-Timer." Hallucinations don't have names, personal histories, or identities as we think of them. Often they accept and adopt any appropriate name given them, such as the folksy Old-Timer. If it will please or beguile the listener, they may make one up and discard it a short while later.

For most persons hallucinations ushered in a host of dreadful experiences. They found that people of this world didn't accept other-world experiences, immediately doubted their sanity, as we have seen, and lost respect for them. They found that the voices could easily gang up on them, literally putting them through hell. As one woman said with great feeling, "You can't have twenty people screaming at you constantly without going to pieces in a little while." Very often alcoholics who have really been living it up find they are tortured by others. Voices come out of ventilators and odd places and comment that the person is a worthless bum that should be killed. One man went through ten days of loud disputes as to how they would kill him. They had a gun—he could hear its hammer fall—a hangman's rope, a flame for burning, etc. This condition is experienced by many alcoholics who finally kill themselves to get it over with. Some patients were brought into an odd drama. One woman found herself being put through some purification ceremonies that resembled events in the Book of Revelation. Another woman underwent surgery so doctors in the other world could do research. Some very inadequate men just went through years of very repetitive criticism. One was criticized five years for a ten-cent bad debt. Others were just told they were worthless, queers, etc. In general, alcoholics find people are talking about them. Schizophrenics find people are talking to them.

Most patients were brought into somewhat sinister relationships. Already estranged from society, they hopefully took up with these promising new friends who talked like kindly helpful people with great powers. Gradually they found their new friends were liars who were more and more critical and tormenting of them. Sometimes voices would play on the patient's guilt. If he didn't do things right, people would be killed somewhere. The next day the voices would refer to news accounts of people's deaths as having been caused by the patient. Often voices would back the patient into a corner where he was doomed if he did or doomed if he didn't do something.

Almost all the patients had tried a series of private maneuvers to get rid of voices. I was especially interested in these because they could suggest effective treatment. Prayer was often tried but to no avail. The very negative voices didn't like religious things, and they could manage to foul up Bible reading or prayers by snatching away thoughts. Patients who tried various ways of placating voices, doing as they suggested, found the voices were taking over and ruining their lives. Many tried vitamins, a change of scenery, various symbolic gestures (i.e., thick padding over the heart, keeping crosses around them, etc.), but these didn't work. They tried to ignore the voices and visions, but it was quite impossible. As one man put it plaintively, "How do you feel when you go to take a leak and find someone else's hand on your cock? There is just no privacy anywhere!" Apparently voices stop only during sleep. They often reappear at the moment of awakening. If they decide to keep one awake, it's good-bye to sleep. Some things did help patients. One woman concluded her unseen lover was really crazy. She counseled him that he really wasn't Jesus Christ, just sick. He seemed to come to his senses gradually and left her. This chain of events started when I first met him. He bragged that he could read my mind. This was so simple to test that I immediately put it to a trial. I would write numbers on a piece of paper and he was to read them. He was a total flop. She began to doubt all her lover's big talk and started treating him until he left! Some patients who had led rather immoral lives found their critical voices gradually came down in volume and left as they vigorously studied the Bible and lived a very moral life.

For reasons that puzzle me, some patients experience only auditory voices, some just visions, others a mix of these. In one man the lower order was voices only, the higher order visual only. It is unknown as to why there are these barriers. I even tried to get one set of voices to do something visual. Try as they might they couldn't do it. Also the "other people" present experience just what the patient experiences. If I showed a patient an ink blot, the voices could see it too. The voices disagreed with one patient's perceptions in the ink blot and chimed in with their own. On repeated tests it appeared they could only see what the patient saw. Moreover, they could only tease the patients about memories that had been recalled when they were present. Prior memories were not available to them until newly recalled by the patient. Apparently they are in definable regions of the mind but don't occupy all of it.

There are two distinct orders of hallucinations. The lower order appears to be much more common (about four to one) than the higher order. Many patients only experience the lower order. Some experience both orders, which must be something like being between heaven and hell. The lower order has *less talent* than the patient. The higher order is *more gifted* than the patient. There are no hallucinations roughly at the patient's own general level of understanding. Any explanation I could give of this would be mere theorizing. The lower order talks a great case but its vocabulary and range of concerns, ideas, and knowledge are less than the patient's. The quotation from Swedenborg at the beginning of this chapter really pertains to the lower order. These hallucinations lie, cheat, deceive, pretend, threaten, etc. Dealing with them is like dealing with very mean drunks. Nothing pleases them. They see the negative side of everything. Catching them in a bold lie doesn't even embarrass them. Their main aim seems to be to live it up at the patient's expense. I asked one lower-order man what his real purposes were. He said, "Fight, screw, win the world." They zero in on every fault or guilt of the patient and play on it. Their general aim seems to be to take over the patient and live through him as they please.

The higher order is just the opposite. Whereas the lower attacks the patient's will, the higher order acts out of great respect for the patient's will. One man experienced the higher order as a sun in the sky at night. When he felt fear of the sun it would withdraw. Even he saw that this was different from "The Bastards." The higher order is highly symbolic. It can produce thousands of complex symbols, many of which have an ancient historical or mythological base. People in the higher order are extremely intuitive of either the patient or anyone else present. I know many won't believe this, but I'll describe it as I found it. They tend to be nonverbal and much more internal, feeling related and subtle.

One of the most gifted of the higher order I met was a beautiful lady who referred to herself as "An Emanation of the Feminine Aspect of the Divine." She was the hallucination in the head of a high school–educated, schizophrenic, not very gifted gas pipefitter. When I first met her she appeared as a spritely little woman, described as very small by the patient, though her size could vary. He had mean critical voices working at him and she came to cheer him up. She played all kinds of entertaining jokes. She was very respectable. The patient had suggested a sexual relationship but she felt it wouldn't be proper. When I asked her a question she could nod yes or no, or yes and no simultaneously. Whenever I or the patient said something very right she would come over to us and hand us her panties. He described her as a most pleasant companion. I first sensed her gift in the form of all the universal symbols she produced. They came so fast that few of them could be described. I recall particularly a Buddhist-type wheel mandala made of intricately woven human bodies that rolled unseen through my office. Some seemed to pertain to ancient myths. I went home and studied some obscure part of Greek myths and asked her about it the next time I saw the gas pipefitter. She not only understood the myth, she saw into its human implications better than I did. When asked, she playfully wrote the Greek alphabet all over the place. The patient couldn't even recognize the letters, but he could copy hers for me.

I first suspected her extrasensory powers from something the patient said. He worked as a plumber's assistant in the hospital. Once, when he got a drink at a fountain, he was surprised to find the water was hot. She explained why. It had something to do with a shower on the other side of the wall, a bypass valve, and differential pressure. The patient told the plumber about this odd set-up. The plumber was surprised. He said it took him two years to figure out why the water was hot sometimes. Once I tried to conceal my mood from the patient and asked her to symbolize it. A very limp penis suddenly turned up in the room —a surprisingly accurate representation of my feelings. When I asked the patient how he saw me he said, "Okay, just average, I guess."

She was the most gifted person in the area of religion I've ever known. She reflected the seriousness of my query. A light question she would answer lightly. The more serious and deep a question, the more depth in her answer. She was entirely unlike talking to earthly theologians who call on history or doctrine to prove a point. She knew the depth of my understanding and led gently into very human allusions that reflected a profound understanding of history. She left soon thereafter when he was transferred to another hospital. The patient didn't understand my conversation with her. He had no religious interests. I remember once his turning in the doorway as he was leaving and asking me to give him a clue as to what she and I had just talked about.

There is no doubt in my mind that some patients are shown things of great importance in hallucinations, though they are not often able to use them. I recall a black, alcoholic burglar who was given a very intimate tour of minority group experiences down through history. Though he was black, he had been shown a very sensitive picture of what it was like to be a Jew, black, Indian, or of another minority group in various cultures down through history. He had seen most of this tour on the floor of the day hall on a back ward. He came out of it feeling he had to do something for minorities, but instead returned to drinking and more bouts of madness.

I recall one woman who had murdered a rather useless husband. In the hospital the Virgin Mary came and counseled her. She was to leave the hospital to drive to the southern part of the state and stand trial for murder. The Virgin had revealed to her that there would be an earthquake here on the day she left and one in the south when she arrived. I was talking to the chaplain late on the day she left and remember very well the brick building swaying. Later I read in the newspapers of an earthquake in the south when she arrived. I wasn't terribly surprised, even though the probability of predicting two separate earthquakes is a bit remote. I guess she had friends in high places. By the way, though the circumstances of the murder could have exonerated her, she chose to plead guilty. She was on some kind of mission for other women in prison.

I was naturally intrigued by the giftedness of the higher order after wrestling with the mean people of the lower order. I found some patients concealed higher-order experiences. They assumed a psychologist would be more interested in the plentiful sexual elements from the lower order. They also feared the power and mystery of the higher order. Often higher values are more repressed than lower values. I couldn't always tell what was higher or lower order. One woman had a group of surgeons doing painful research on her joints for the welfare of mankind. I tested their knowledge and found it to be far less than the patient's. They were fakes of the lower order. Still, she chose to stay with them in case her years of pain could prevent arthritis in later life. One naturally meets Jesus Christ in this inner world. Fake Christs of the lower order are easy to see through. They brag about their powers and the wonders they can do. When criticized they easily become defensive and threatening. The real Christlike figures from the higher order are just the opposite. They often say nothing, yet their radiant presence has an intense effect on the patient. They lead gently with a profound understanding of the patient's inner potentials. They do good. I encouraged the man with a sun from the higher order to try to get acquainted with it. With some justification he had concealed the sun from me. As he joined with the sun he went through a series of religious experiences that required temporary seclusion and supervision. He had been a prison tough guy and numinous religious experience was a bit much for him. He trembled and wept when recalling these experiences even days later. He went down a tunnel in the ground until he came to doors holding creatures in hell. He was tempted to open the doors when a powerfully impressive Christlike figure, all in radiant white, stopped him. Just looking into the figure's eyes had a profound influence on him. He knew he was understood and loved. He knew this figure was wiser than him. The figure guided him out into the daylight. There he saw a gigantic golden trumpet that signaled he was to become musical. He did. He wrote about four songs a day and kept two other patients busy writing down the music, since he didn't know how. He appeared to have recovered and left the hospital. I would have some reservations about how well he would be in the future. It was a bit of a jump for a tough crook to suddenly change so much. The values of the higher order require some time to really integrate into one's life.

Many patients complained about extrasensory experiences in their hallucinations. They served merely to frighten the patient. A man was about to go to a dance and a giant cut glass punch bowl descended from the ceiling. It was seen later at the dance. Voices described what other patients were going to do and the patients proceeded to do them. A man was given a written order for some pipe fittings. Later the order disappeared. A few minutes later the same stranger came with the same written order. This time it stayed. One patient complained bitterly about voices reading off her opponents cards in a card game. It spoiled the game. She had to quit cards. ESP in the realm of hallucinations seems quite variable. Lower-order figures often claim to have the power and don't have it. Higher-order figures seem to have ESP powers. Unfortunately ESP just seems to frighten the patient further. I've not heard of any instance where a patient could make any constructive use of it.

Apparently it is quite possible for a person to have sexual intercourse with hallucinations. One woman described it as being more inward and much nicer than having a real man. Also, hallucinations can get sick just as a person does. For several days the "Old-Timer" had a bad cold he couldn't shake. The patient could hear it in his voice. At the time the patient himself felt fine. It is of course a little puzzling to find hallucinations themselves can get sick.

Hallucinations were very clearly the basis for delusional ideas. As the patient dealt more and more with the "other world," even his vocabulary would change. Symbolic phrases that were learned there became a part of the patient's vocabulary. A whole set of ideas from the other world would be adopted, leaving the person technically delusional. It is hardly possible for an individual to experience a strange new world of

148

experience some sixteen hours a day without it gradually coloring his whole view of reality.

Occasionally I could see some relationship between the individual and his hallucinations. Persons who had violated their own conscience seemed to be mercilessly tortured by consciencelike lower-order figures. A figure from the higher order suggested to me that the function of the lower order was basically to illustrate one's faults. One couldn't help but feel that ten or twenty years of illustration was excessive. Repressed, "good" people were often tormented with sexual fantasies. One woman seemed almost saintly in her behavior. She had the dirtiest voices I had ever known. She didn't feel comfortable even repeating the language they used. Conversely, some people who had been criminals had spiritually elevated hallucinations from the higher order. One man had religious visions in solitary confinement that many ministers would give their left hand to have. Inadequate people had even more inadequate hallucinations, such as the man who just heard "Hey" for years. One man who was plagued by radiation from other people's eyes clearly needed to be close to others but couldn't handle tender feelings.

Rarely I could break through a hallucination. A man came in complaining that he had a woman's breast for several days. It flopped around and got in his way as he worked. I asked for a description of this breast I couldn't see. One teat was pendulous and poorly shaped. The other had a youthful, more impressive shape. He associated an old girlfriend with the pendulous one and a new girl friend with the more pointed breast. I asked if he were caught between girl friends. He was. He felt obligations to the old one and desire for the new one. I suggested that he make up his mind between them. It's easy to guess he chose the new one. With this decision the hallucinated breasts disappeared. The breasts seemed to represent his being plagued by an ambivalence that he hadn't faced and worked out.

I also found that patients frequently misunderstood what their own voices were talking about. One man had voices purporting to come from Washington, D.C. They also printed U.S. on a lot of things. At first I quizzed them on their knowledge of the city itself. They didn't know anything about it. Finally I asked if they were from the city in the eastern part of the United States or did they mean they were at the seat of government of the patient. They said they were at the patient's inner seat of government. Hallucinations are symbolic of inner states and experiences of the patient. The higher order is clearly aware of this. The patients make the same mistake everyone else would make of thinking that ordinary language has ordinary referents. When voices say something is poisonous, they mean it is bad for the patient, but not literally poisonous. One woman had voices saying that she should suck her son's pickle (penis). This went on for months. She was very upset at this insulting suggestion. She became violent and broke windows trying to stop the voices. It took some talking with them to get the message translated. The message gradually clarified and the voices faded. The final message was: love and take care of your son. She had an inadequate husband who was jealous of a new son. She chose to neglect the son to try to preserve the marriage and ended up shooting the husband in the midst of madness. The voices were trying to reestablish her love relationship to her son. When she recognized and accepted this the voices stopped and never returned. I don't really know why the inner is so symbolic. The problem is similar to the question of why dreams are symbolic.

Many patients indicated that the voices were trying to gain control of a part of them. In one the voices worked for years to get control of an eye. They did, and the eye actually went out of normal alignment. Several had voices trying to get their hearing. If they did, the patient would become noticeably hard of hearing. I've seen voices seize the tongue and speak through the person. All this was rather startling. The patients were speaking of what is described in ancient literature as possession. Often there was a long battle, with the patient gradually becoming possessed. There were many very psychotic patients around who looked like they had become totally possessed. I recall examining one man who professed to being moral and upright. In a few minutes the dirtiest talk would come from his mouth, mostly about assholes. I would remind him of his morality. Yes, yes, he would say, he was very careful to always think clean thoughts. In the next minute he rambled on about menstrual cloths. It looked as if he were possessed and there was just a fragment of the original man present.

The talk about possession led me back into the ancient literature. Could modern patients totally removed in time and experience from the ancients be describing essentially the same terms. There were mostly fragments in the Bible and in later old texts. The most careful and detailed description of the spiritual world was to be found in the works of Swedenborg, written about two centuries ago. Swedenborg was a noted scientist who explored inner states until he broke through into the spiritual world. His careful findings were set down in detail.[2] I carefully compared what he and these patients had to say.[3] Separated by two centuries and with very different backgrounds, the patients and Swedenborg were describing the same realm. The lower order he called hell and the higher order heaven. Swedenborg's description threw light on several puzzling aspects of hallucinations. Spirits in hell are more limited and for spiritual reasons they don't have a personal identity as we know it. They do want to possess and control persons. Angels in heaven are very rich in their understanding and perception. The common contemporary explanation for hallucinations is that they are eruptions from the unconscious. This doesn't quite explain the giftedness of "An Emanation of the Feminine Aspect of the Divine" nor does it explain a lot of other aspects. We will come back to this later, but for the present my guess is that the explanation via the unconscious and the spiritual world are essentially the same thing. The spiritual world is normally unconscious. Swedenborg implied it was very dangerous to break into this realm, and my patients would agree with him.

I don't wish to imply that hallucinations are fully understood. There is probably much more that could be learned from this realm even though I believe the above is a roughly accurate phenomenological map. Moreover hallucinations are not easy to treat.

The whole treatment of hallucinations could perhaps be summed up in a few words. When the patient was coming to have an abnormal dependency on hallucinations, I would try to break the relationship. This occurred when I showed a woman her lover didn't really have ESP. In general the lower-order hallucinations are the most difficult to deal with. When the patient is really tormented it pays to relieve the pressure by administering ataratic drugs (i.e., thorazine). Drugs don't stop the hallucinations but they do lessen the patient's reaction to them. But when the patient is working out material in psycho-therapy, drugs should be stopped or used in limited amounts. The painful struggle is more help to psychotherapy than a drugged detachment.

There should be some use in the patient learning from the lower order as an illustration of his individual weaknesses and tendencies, though I have not yet seen this work. Higher-order hallucinations do appear more treatable. The patient can be helped to overcome the fear of these higher values and be guided in exploring and integrating them. The therapist may well be surprised at their power as they approach conscious-ness. On a few occasions I was able to get a patient to unite with the higher values. The person became grossly disturbed for several days as the higher values blasted through his consciousness. Then he needed help to understand, accept, and live by these new values. The more capable the patient, the easier the task. It is very like new wine in old bottles. Where the bottle is too limited, it is best to keep new wine out of it.

For the most part this is a relatively little-known realm. In its symbolism and gross contours it doesn't look too strange to those who have explored fantasy, the hypnogogic, and dreams. The new element may be the relative impairment of individuals who have full psychotic hallucinations. They are not equipped to be plagued by more than even gifted normals could really understand.

If nothing else, I would like to leave you with some feeling of sympathy for people faced with unseen, doggedly persistent torturers, people who lose all privacy and refuge, who are shown wonders that simply frighten them. I would also like to leave open the real question of what it all means, even though I am plagued by the similarity of this realm and what has been described as heaven and hell.

11

Mystical Experience:
The Flowering of Understanding

. . . . The Lord is The Only Man. . . .
Emanuel Swedenborg, *Arcana Coelestia* (¶ 2996), 1749–1756

I have heard that churches which are in different goods and truths
. . . are like so many gems in a King's crown.
Emanuel Swedenborg, *True Christian Religion* (¶ 763), 1771

In our descent into the natural depth in man we have been
pretty clearly within the realm of the personal psyche, though
in dreams and even more in hallucinations we began to see
intimations of a beyond. In mystical experience the limited self
is opened up, revealing a beyond with a host of new meanings.
In mystical experience is the ultimate that the individual can
discover. Though it has a considerable range of depths, there is
no higher, no deeper, no greater experience than what is found
in the surprising union of the individual with his fundamental
source.

The mystical is itself a somewhat confused, cloudy area, so

much so that the word mystical can mean unclear. For honest and sensible reasons many will feel that mystical experiences are not real. They have not experienced anything like it so the reports of mystics naturally look like pretense, fancy, or nonsense. Let me say most firmly that it seems quite reasonable to me for persons to not believe what has not been seen, felt, or experienced. I would just ask those without such experience to look tolerantly at the accounts of ordinary people who have.

I hesitate to describe this region more than any other for a host of reasons. In this area we look at man's most sacred experiences. For personal reasons I am loath to do anything that seems to tinker with what another person considers sacred. The feeling of sacredness arises from the innermost of individuals. I would respect even the objects a primitive considers sacred. It is a very personal, private area of the most significant feelings.

A worse danger is that we touch on realms that are normally considered religious. Some grow deaf and irritated at the mere mention of this. Religion is a terrible baggage of nonsense for them. To them it looks like weak-minded people's wishful thinking. This negativism is easily understood and dealt with. They have seen no God to fear. Quite a bit worse are the endless disputes among the religious, who all represent their approach as the one true religion. Most difficult of all are the well-trained religious who lack any personal mystical experiences. They attack with the intellect, justifying themselves with chapter and verse. It will be seen that this experience points quite beyond sectarian disputes to a more peaceful understanding.

Another difficulty with this area is that it becomes confused with human pride. Who has the biggest vision; who is the master, the true guru? The disputes are not among the real mystics. They can see the similarity in each other. The debates arise at a lower level, among followers or pretenders to wisdom. Some people came considerable distances to impress me with their visions, the auras they could see, etc. It is a little distressing to find even this area confused with human pride. It was a different matter when they came asking for help to understand their experiences.

The mysticism to be dealt with here is a distillation of the experiences of many. The basis of this whole presentation remains the phenomenological description of human experience, just as it has been from the beginning. Whatever is in human experience can be described, even if it is odd, surprising, and controversial.

Perhaps my experience in speaking to small groups on mysticism will help clarify some of the basic human difficulties in communication in this area. I found it best to elicit each one's personal experiences first. We then had a healthier basis on which to compare notes. If I just rambled on about the shape of my or another's mystical experience some were fascinated and some were irritated and even inflamed. To those without parallel experiences it quite reasonably sounded like pretentious hogwash. The spirit of the initial sharing put us roughly on the same human ground even though we differed widely in what had actually been experienced. On this common ground as persons, it became quite apparent that the man with little or no experience had as many rights as the one with an abundance of experience. We were all equally human and this somehow is what the mystical thing is all about.

The Range of Mystical Experiences

The most common mystical experience is, oddly enough, simply experiencing anything—brushing one's teeth, eating a meal, or walking down the street. Any ordinary experience. In some real ways this is the most profound of all the possible mystical experiences though it is rarely appreciated as such. The problem is that we are too used to it. It is so common. What is missing is amazement at the mystery of ordinary existence.

Suppose you had just this moment been born as a full-fledged adult, with your present mind and understanding. You would be absolutely stunned at the things and people around you. Most of the day would be taken up with "ohs" and "ahs" as you went around feeling things. It would be a frightfully impressive and awesome mystical experience. You would be stunned by the beauty of simple things such as the graceful form of plants. This is one of the hallmarks of the mystical experience, to find things fantastically beautiful and good just as they are. This comes before eating the apple of the tree of knowledge of good and evil (Gen. 2:17). After the apple we doubt, question, evaluate, quibble, and lose the primitive sense of awe. It is quite probable that infants outdistance adults in this simple capacity. We seem to see it in the infant's total body excitement at seeing what is to our more enlightened and jaded eyes simply a cheap plastic gadget.

In Zen Buddhism a seeker asks to learn of the Buddha and the master scoops up a handful of flax seed as a perfectly adequate answer. The student's mind is beclouded by information. "That is, of course, merely flax seed—maybe it's symbolic of something." No. Not symbolic. Literally the Buddha. The Buddha is everything. If you do not appreciate anything of everything, how can you find the Buddha?

The lowest level of mystical experience lies in finding some degree of awe at the mere presence of existence. If you want, it lies in a childlike capacity to be impressed by things, be they flax seed, man, cities, clouds, or remote stars. The root of the experience is to be impressed with things just as they are. Some find this bit of awe easiest in the presence of nature. But it is also possible with even the simplest things made by man. Can you patiently look at a greasy discarded auto part and see the endless workers whose lives led to that product? Can you see in it the impressive will of man to make things go, to do new things? One mystic, Jacob Böhme, fell into an awesome reverence for all things while looking at the play of light on a pewter dish.

There are several relatively consistent aspects to this lowest level of mystical experience. The individual feels in accord with things and gives time to a relaxed perception of things. It is characteristically an unhurried experience. The individual notes very fine details of objects or people. It is not based on overlooking reality but on seeing it unusually well. There is little of the subject/object split. That is, the individual feels with what was perceived. When looking at a graceful plant he feels graceful. The experience has clear aesthetic overtones. Things are beautiful in an artistic sense. Those who enjoy the arts readily enjoy this kind of experience. Aesthetic experience itself is a lower level of what will be described here as mystical experience. There may not be any revelation content to the experience. The real meaning may lie simply in one's accord with the real beauty of existence. Or the substance of the experience may hint at meanings beyond this. The individual may feel the wonder of existence in a single plant or may sense the Creator of existence. This addition of meaning can be seen two ways. Those who are really aesthetically inclined may see the added meaning as the individual's own contamination of the beauty of things seen. Conversely, others would feel the basic aesthetic experience to be the entrance to broader meanings. I don't think it important to set values one way or the other. They reflect basic differences in individual approaches to reality.

It is difficult and perhaps not entirely appropriate to set a total rank ordering to mystical experiences, but the love between individuals is another example of lower-level and relatively common mystical experience. There is the same joy at seeing the loved one. The I/you split is overcome to varying degrees. The one loved and one's self are somehow one life. The sacraments of marriage and, indeed, sexual experience with the loved one, has the same implications of overcoming duality. In some inner way the lovers experience their relationship as a one. It is somewhat painful for lovers when duality returns and each finds their fundamental differences from the other. It would be easy to say that lovers each project their unconscious potentials into each other and are trying to unite with themselves in their loved one. This sounds like a nice psychological explanation, but lovers would feel it overlooks the nature of the experience of love itself. Those who freely engage in sex outside of love are, in effect, throwing out the baby and keeping the bath. It is the love between individuals that makes their sexual experience so impressive and not vice versa. Lovers can have a tremendous experience by just holding hands.

Human love is not ordinarily seen as part of the whole continuum of mystical experiences. It has the same marks. It is an unhurried experience of great beauty. It overcomes the split between the individual and others. It is awesome in its power. It may or may not inform itself with the meaning of existence. The experience itself may be the answer to all its own questions. Or lovers may feel creatively united to all creation. In primitive ceremonies lovers might make love in the furrow of a plowed field to fertilize the whole field. They feel fertile with each other and feel part of creating. And indeed this fertility would create a home and often the lives of other persons. The creating power of love is not evanescent or theoretical. The individual who loves making things creates better things. The carpenter who loves woodwork builds a better house. The medieval guilds dealt with a man's love in terms of the work of his trade. By our haste and emphasis on the amount of production we have somewhat lost sight of this root of great craftsmanship. In Zen Buddhism it is well known that mystical enlightenment is possible through simple craftsmanship, whether it be in making pots, arranging flowers, drawing words on paper, or swordsmanship.

In the tradition of the samurai, the swordsman who had become one with his sword was very dangerous, since he was beyond living or dying. Ordinary swordsmen still felt *they* controlled the *sword*, and they very much feared dying. The great potter or painter molded his spirit into his art to such an extent that works of the master could be recognized by experts centuries later.

The Horrible Satori

The next level of enlightenment is ushered in by an even greater degree of loss of ego-awareness. The ordinary individual who stumbles into this realm may well find himself terrified. He may feel like he is dying or completely losing his mind. The result is a horrible, half-born satori. I prefer the Japanese term satori to the more Western enlightenment. Enlightenment we apply to anything a little better than the average; a cigarette ad can be enlightened. Satori is an uncommon but normal experience. Awareness of one's self as an individual temporarily disappears and there follows a spontaneous blossoming of awareness of the real nature of creation. The gate to satori is through the death of self (John 3:3).

I have run into difficulties in getting through the death of the self in several aspects of my clinical experience. In the early sixties a few clinicians were involved with aiding individuals to have direct mystical experiences through the legal use of psychedelic drugs such as LSD, mescaline, psilocybin, etc. This was before the black market sale of these drugs led to their infamy and legal suppression. Actually I am now for their suppression, or at best their use only under well-controlled conditions.

We were operating under the general thesis that individuals who had massive mystical experiences gained a broadened meaning to their life. This was considered therapeutic in a higher sense than simply removing pathology. Through a great deal of experimentation on ourselves and others there gradually evolved agreement among the experts in this realm. I was struck by the fact that what we had evolved was essentially what primitive groups (i.e., with no written language) all over the world had evolved in their use of psychedelic drugs. The enlightened drug experience given by primitives required a number of psychological safeguards. It was given only to adults, on a serious quest, after much internal preparation. The preparation might involve withdrawal, fasting, prayer, etc., whatever was preparatory in that culture. The drug was considered a sacred substance given only by a priest (shaman, etc.) of that culture who had considerable drug experience himself. Though the substances were freely growing around them, the sacred substance was only given under sacred circumstances; it wasn't for careless chewing at any time. The seeker was surrounded and protected by the ancient symbols of his culture. The American Indian peyotists are an example of this kind of culture.

In our research we evolved much the same kind of practice. The patient had to be on a serious quest, under the guidance of a person experienced with the drug. We were quite aware that the selection of the individual and his careful preparation was part of the quality of the results. The individual was encouraged to dwell on the things of concern to him while under the drug. Because of the general looseness and variability in our culture our results were probably somewhat inferior to what the primitives obtained.

With these safeguards intense mystical enlightenment was certainly possible and even relatively common.[1] The only debate among the experts was whether the ego-awareness should be blasted out of existence by high doses or whether the individual should be encouraged to learn his way around selfhood on lower doses.

We stumbled into a whole new area of human experience. Selfhood was palpably an obstacle to the mystical experience. Some foundered on this border to enlightenment, producing a terrifying experience later described by illegal drug users as a "bad trip." It was critical that the guide spot the hang-up and be able to guide the individual around it. Examples will illustrate this.

Under LSD one woman was feeling everything move. Inwardly she hung on with fear and began to feel sick. She was encouraged to go with the movement. In moments she broke into a world of beautiful religious images. Another man was on the edge of losing personal identity. With a worried look he said over and over, "Who is so-and-so?"—his own name. It wasn't until the issue of name/identity became inconsequential that he got beyond this. Another young woman fought the gradual loss of identity. She felt she was undergoing slow surgery that was cutting off pieces of herself. In the final cutting apart of her heart she died and suddenly awoke joyfully to the One life. One man on the way to becoming all things illustrated the difference between the ordinary view and satori. He said, "You name it, I'll be it." Several simply felt they were dying. They were inclined to try to sit up, try to be alert, stay alive. To relax into an experience of themselves was to die. The guide had to have enough confidence and experience to encourage the individual to relax, give up, and die. To be near the dissolution of self was a terrifying experience. The individual feared the loss of all he knew and the entering of a dark, numinous, frightening unknown. For some the experience was mostly a threatening dissolution with just a bare hint of what awaited them. Ideas of death or madness were common. There was more horror than satori.

Later I discovered very similar examples in individuals without any use of drugs. A person would present complaints of a repetitive nightmare or frightening daytime experiences. He

162

had to be guided through the experience to find what was hidden it it. Again there were the same signs of dissolution of the self and satori when the self perished. One man had been mercilessly depth-charged in a submarine and had nightmares after that for a long while. In the nightmare he was hanging on to life. He was encouraged to go through the whole destruction of the submarine and of himself. He broke through into intensely beautiful experiences that told him of the real meaning and purpose of life. One woman had nearly choked to death as an infant. She was aided to experience both her dying and her subsequent enlightenment. The early trauma had left her permanently afraid and attracted to the experience. One young man had fallen into enlightenment at age seven. He was hiding from a disturbed noisy household behind a chair. He sat for a long time in an odd position until his legs were numb. Suddenly he fell into a trance. There was the Lord God of heaven. The Lord created earth as represented by a beach scene. He was the Lord, which was the scene, which was in the position in which he sat. Instead of being an intensely pleasurable experience, the seven-year-old boy came out of it badly shaken, fearing for his sanity.

I gradually learned to suspect some sort of borderline enlightenment whenever a traumatic experience was involved. Once you knew the individual had stumbled near enlightenment, it was easy to close the ring. They could be encouraged to go through the experience and savor what was on the other side. They had to be counseled that the apparently oad experience of satori was very ancient and much sought after. The individual had some follow-up work to do to integrate the new meanings into his experience.

I don't know how generally true this insight is, but I would not be terribly surprised if it were eventually found that this borderline, horrible satori was the root of all psychopathology.

Satori Itself

The way into satori is quite clear. It is along the lines of the lower levels of mystical experience itself. Instead of departing from reality, the individual enters into it more fully. There is an unhurried full feeling with and appreciation of ordinary things just as they are. The conceptual barriers between the self and others and self and things dissolves. There is a growing feeling of Oneness. This Oneness is alive, real, and immediately present. There may or may not be a feeling that one is dying or dissolving. There is forgetfulness of self. Suddenly there is a breakthrough into pure feeling/understanding.

Experiences at this level can range from a peaceful unity of all things to the appearance of the Lord Himself. The Lord appears as tremendously intense love, knowing, all there is. If there is any trace of awareness of self the Lord may appear in the zenith of the individual and unite with the individual in the *unio mystica*. All personal values are suddenly shattered. There is only God. The One and Only then shows Itself through all the levels of creation. With painful love the One chooses to create Itself into the individual who gradually awakens again as a person. There are secret understandings exchanged between the One and the individual. The stunned individual gradually returns again to personal awareness. It is not uncommon for the individual to be dreadfully disappointed at finding himself alive again in the ordinary world. The whole inner values of the person have been turned around.

This is the big satori, the ultimate, highest experience possible to the individual. Obviously the loss of selfhood cannot be made by the individual. It and satori are given by grace. The knowledge gained in satori is noetic; that is, it is given as fully true. There is no possibility of even questioning it until the little self appears. At the time it is given there is no individual around to doubt it. The general understanding given is that there is only One. The One is pleased to experience itself through all possible orders of creation. Being all that is, It cannot but create all that is. It experiences Itself on all levels. Out of love it creates Itself as creation and suffers Itself through all possible orders and limitations of creation. The individual is the One in limited form, seeking its way back to Itself. The individual, all creation, and the One are the same. The purpose of creation is that the One playfully experience all its possibilities, so to speak, just to pass the time. Each individual is a possibility that leads back to the One.

Back to Earth

The total implications of satori are too vast to be neatly summarized since it comprises the most essential insight of all religions. I wish to remain within the realm of human experience and merely attempt to establish a number of facts about this most numinous, surprising, and controversial level of experience.

Judging from contact with a wide variety of people under psychedelic drugs, in anesthesia, in madness and normality, satori in some degree is relatively common.[2] It has been given and probably will be given to many. If the lesser levels of what is described here as mystical experience are included, then probably no one has been fully excluded. The big satori, in which personal identity is totally lost for a while and only God exists, seems uncommon but not rare. Satori does not seem to be limited to individuals of any particular station of life, culture, religion, or time. It has occurred to prisoners in solitary confinement, to isolated explorers, to madmen, and to ordinary housewives. A more fundamental issue is in the fruit it bears in the life of the person. I have known madmen who saw the devil in much the same way that Jesus did during his forty days in the desert. But there is considerable difference in the quality of these men and of the ultimate fruits of the vision.

Satori may give new life to the individual's original religious beliefs or establish a feeling for a universality that transcends individual religions. It can do both. The religion is strengthened and is seen as really talking about the universal.

It is very curious to me that the religious have as much difficulty with mystical experiences as psychologists do, if not more. Most religions imply that the great vision has been given to their prophet in the remote past and that no really great vision is to be expected until the judgment day. This makes the experience remote, other-worldly, and mostly unattainable. Most religious leaders have had no mystical experience. They are disturbed by reports of it in others and often give it little or no credence whether or not the one reporting it is within their own faith. Some religions have as their main purpose the development of direct individual experience of the divine. Hindu Yoga and Zen Buddhism are notable examples of this. If the yogi comes out of a trance and says in a stunned way that he is Brahma, other adepts in this faith are pleased that another has found the way. They gather around and seek to learn from him rather than rush for a straight jacket. These religions are extremely psychological. Their exercises involve a descent into depth that provides personal psychological insight and growth whether or not the big satori seizes the individual. All religions seem to involve this kind of element more or less; it is simply clearer and more direct in some. In others the descent into depth is complexly and remotely symbolized as in most of Christianity. Some contemplative Christians enter on the same path followed by the religions that involve a personal descent into depth. Swedenborg, St. Francis of Assisi, and St. Theresa are just a few Christian examples.

What makes Swedenborg striking is that he recorded almost every detail of what he found in his personal journey in about forty volumes. He felt that instead of remaining in remote symbols, the whole thing should be made as clear, direct, and understandable as possible. In fact, he may be the most completely and explicitly detailed of all the mystics. Though he looks clearly Christian, one can easily discern that what he was talking about transcended sectarian differences. For instance, he dropped a casual remark that the blacks of Africa were favored in heaven because they were easily instructed by angels. In the 1700s their religion was un-Christian, primitive animism. It had in it the seeds of heavenly understanding.

That satori can occur under psychedelic drugs or anesthesia will disturb some. It looks at first sight as if a fake enlightenment is being manufactured by a chemical change in the brain. I don't think so. In both cases sensation is cut off and the person is drawn inward into the most essential levels of his self. What is accomplished chemically is the most fundamental goal of yogis and the contemplative religions. Satori is not invariable under any given chemical conditions. Nor is it always rememberable. And of course the fruits of satori, which is its final, ultimate proof, don't always follow. My guess is that the chemical aspects of satori merely help clarify what needs to be accomplished inwardly to get beyond selfhood. The cardinal message of satori itself, given under any circumstances, is that it is not the individual's own limited will that is operating. It also seems clear that the individual who finds his way into satori without drugs probably is more advanced as a person than the one swept into it through anesthesia. This is probably why Hindu leaders banned drug use in ancient times even though they seemed to be aware of its religious potential. In modern times the Maharishi and others have banned drug use by followers for similar reasons.

For many the implications of the mystical insight raise more questions than answers. What does it do for the individual? This very much depends on how the person sees it and uses it. One man who found it impossible to believe in God went through the great enlightenment and came back with the distinct impression there really was One, and this One was pure energy. God, Christ, and all religious ideas were put aside. Some are merely disturbed in their beliefs by such an experience. Some come back with the feeling they are literally the One Life and they carry this into action by caring for others. This is the ultimate meaning of the Golden Rule. You are the one that you take care of.

In some real sense satori or enlightenment itself is merely pretty flowers in the air until it is made to bear fruit in one's actions. Its ultimate worth is in the fruit it bears, and the fruit is the good done for the environment or for others.

Does satori give the individual any special advantage? Not really. It is said that God tries those he loves the most. Christ's episode on Golgotha is an example. A Zen monk was asked what comes after enlightenment. His answer was that one chopped wood and carried water. That is, one did the necessary tasks at hand. One monk had enlightenment while he cleaned toilets in a monastery. Though he became the abbot he chose to keep the toilet-cleaning task. There are some advantages of satori. The individual no longer fears death. The One cannot die. It can only go through apparent transformations. Also, the person who has enjoyed satori no longer feels he is alone in a machinelike universe of chance. The whole universe is a living presence. Can the enlightened one brag at having had the big picture? Not really. It would be more accurate for the person to say he has been had by enlightenment. The individual is had, in all kinds of senses.

One drawback of small satories is that the individual may go through a painful effort to get back to the peace of heaven. I know one woman who was had by enlightenment during childbirth. She tried to conceive another child on the same day, to carry it the same period, with the same doctor, just to get back to the original experience; she failed. One cannot manufacture enlightenment by any combination of circumstances. This would encroach on God's freedom, which is impossible. Even with the careful use of LSD we found we were merely maximizing the possibility. Whether it was given or not was beyond our choice.

Is the full enlightened one someone special? Hardly, since even bums and psychotics may have a glimpse of the big picture. The person is special only insofar as his fruits are special. Enlightenment doesn't even mean that the person should go out and save the world. The fully enlightened janitor may just do his job very well and be a nice person to have around. In a cosmic sense this may really be the fruit sent from heaven.

People often wonder how enlightenment can jibe with war, poverty, death, and disease. These things make them feel there must not be anyone up there, or that the Creator has a touch of human meanness. What God did to Jesus didn't seem like the act of a kindly father.

The best answer to this I have seen is in the Hindu *Bhagavad Gita*, in which Arjuna represents every man.[3] Arjuna is by birth a warrior, engaged in a war against his own brothers. He is speaking to Krishna, who is God incarnate. Arjuna asks Krishna if he can get out of this painful role of having to fight and kill his own brothers. Krishna enlightens Arjuna to the effect that first Arjuna should get over the idea that anyone dies! Everyone/Arjuna has to see into the vast implications of this before he sees it is right and proper that each carry out the duties that befall him, however mean they are. Many Christians can see the paradoxical beauty in a kindly father executing Jesus: a few hours of pain to give birth to good for countless thousands down through history. All the negatives come from too limited a view of the total situation. From the viewpoint of the Divine it is indeed all good. From our limited viewpoint it doesn't look nearly as good. In fact, it may look rather terrible. That there is no real death takes some sting out of existence and radically shifts its meaning. Death in a spiritual sense means to miss the real point or truth of existence. Hence when someone chose to leave friends (who were alive in a material sense) and follow Christ, Christ referred to the friends as dead (Luke 9:60). These dead are, of course, capable of rebirth. Curiously enough the same symbolic language that appears in the hypnogogic, dreams, and hallucinations also reappears in the spiritual realm. Swedenborg was studying his own dreams when he penetrated the dense forest of biblical symbolism.[4] A person while in satori asked the Lord of death. The Lord answered, "What death? I know of no death"—a lofty view indeed and not that of ordinary persons.

Summary

The lowest and ever-present level of mystical experience is real ordinary experiencing. It breaks through into mysticism when the individual feels awe at the simple presence of existence.

Another common level of the mystical is human love. This presages the hallmarks of the mystical, that the duality of self and other is overcome in a unity that is impressive in its love and goodness.

The borderline of more profound mystical experience requires the dissolving of personal identity. Many seem caught at this border in fear of death or madness that is a horrible, half-born satori.

The death of the self is the birth of all else. In varying degrees the individual experiences the essential truth that is reflected in different ways in the many religions.

This experience is relatively commonly given to people in

170

various times, places, circumstances, cultures, and religions.

In even a mystical sense the critical issue is what fruit the experience bears in the individual's life. The fruit is its substantiality.

12

Implications of the Descent into Depth

There was a numerous crowd of spirits about me that sounded like a disorderly stream. They were complaining that everything was going to destruction; for nothing in the crowd appeared organized, and this made them fear destruction. They also supposed that it would be total destruction, as is the case in such circumstances. But in the midst of them I perceived a soft sound, angelically sweet, suggesting nothing but order. Angelic choirs were there within, and the disorderly crowd of spirits was without. This angelic strain continued a long time; and I was told that it betokened how the Lord rules confused and disorderly exteriors from what is peaceful in their midst, regulating the disorders in the circumference, by restraining each from the error of its own nature.
Emanuel Swedenborg, *Arcana Coelestia* (¶ 5396), 1749–1756

We have surveyed a number of aspects of psyche, mind, or man's experiencing. Our mode has been mainly phenomenology: the attempt to capture and describe things as they are. This survey has been necessarily somewhat brief. Man's experience and mind itself is of limitless expanse. Studies of certain regions, such as dreams, already fill hundreds of volumes. Some might wish to explore hallucinations or mystical experience more. Yet what has been said of these regions probably has been representatively accurate. The areas studied have been arranged in a rough order from what is our most common, conscious, external experience to inner, rarer, and more puzzling kinds of experience. If we left the whole matter at this point there would be too many puzzling loose ends. These varied levels show a consistent trend, and by bringing it out the whole will be knit together. What is natural and consistent in man will become more apparent. Whereas before we were mainly describing and grouping similar descriptions, now we permit greater speculation in order to attempt to reach beyond many details to the underlying natural consistencies.

It is more comfortable to describe areas of human experience, even if it is weird, strange experience. Speculating and theory-building looks dangerous to me. If someone asked me what my greatest disappointment is in the science of psychology, I would answer that psychology has largely overlooked gentle human experience in favor of a Babel of theories that contribute very little to our understanding. This bias has thrown out whole areas of human experience. The hypnogogic is barely known. It is easy to turn up fascinating findings in hallucinations that are so unknown to psychologists most would not believe them. And satori—! But I will permit myself to speculate and conceive theory, as long as it accords with what has been observed of human experience. First experience, then guesses.

The Natural Consistency in the Descent

The surface man talks to himself, observes the world, deals with others, does things, and is proud of himself as Mr. or Ms. so-and-so. This is almost all that many people know of themselves. The grave mysteries of ordinary experience are taken for granted. How do we move our hands, how does thought form? Well, everyone knows—it just does.

The description of the complexities of seeing and hearing other persons is a beginning of the descent into one's own depth. To really feel, see, and hear another requires a careful search of your own feelings. To really feel what it is like to be an aged man one must become in some way that aged man. It is easiest to play with children if one becomes childlike. The loosening up of this capacity to be like others, to feel others, loosens up the conception of one's self. It tends to diminish the boundaries between self and others that is perhaps the most critical of all personal limitations. The simple exercise of feeling like others reflects in dreams in which parts of the self are seen as others. It culminates in the mystical insight in which the individual finds he is all life. Madness is the opposite of joining with others. Within madness are all the degrees of isolation and cutting off, both from others and from one's self.

Incidentally, it very early became apparent to me that what the individual does to himself, he tries to do to others. Self/others are the same in some way. The person who represses inner feeling tends to have the same effect on others. In madness, isolation from one's own natural trends and capacities is also isolation from the natural world. The moralist, who is in grave battle to put down his own instincts, would like to see all signs of instinct in the world covered up because they are so dreadfully apparent and suggestive (to him). One woman was hospitalized because she beat up strangers in passing cars. The naughty strangers were shifting gears in sexually suggestive ways. The man who cheats himself finds the world remarkably untrustworthy. The holy man finds holiness suggested everywhere. Inside equals outside. In dreams, fantasy, meditation, etc., the inside is easily experienced as outside. That is why concentration on even a tiny outside point can produce a sensitive picture of inside trends. In madness the relationship to the inside is disturbed, hence the relationship to the outside is disturbed. In hallucinations the inside is literally seen and heard as outside. In the mystical opening of the innermost of man is found the whole of creation. I have often thought that one way to go into the world was to go into one's own depths. Or, one way to understand the inside was precisely to be attentive to what was outside. Once, when feeling very distraught, I turned to chopping wood as though the wood would teach me and straighten out my feelings. I slammed the ax down on the first log, trying to split it. The wood reminded me that I had to be very attentive to knots and its grain. In effect it said, "I will split if you are considerate of my nature." I have become quite accustomed to the inside/outside equivalence, so much so that I am no longer sure that they are separate realms.

If I had to define the relationship between inside and outside, my guess would be that they are two aspects of the same. And, paradoxically, I would say the reality of the inner is outside, and the reality of the outer is inside. To explain, one can't really undo madness just by rearranging the inside. It is easier to do it from outside. This has implications beyond showing madmen how to become productive again. Even Freud concentrated on the transference: what the person does with others. The modern psychotherapies are drifting clearly toward what a person does right here and now. All this suggests the reality of the inner disturbances is outer, in behavior, in what a person does.

But the opposite is also true: the reality of a beautiful painting on the outside, for instance, is inner. That is, to learn to enjoy art, one needs to learn to pick up inner feelings stirred by the art. I don't think aesthetics is merely a nice thing to have around to decorate the environment. If everyone really appreciated art we would have people more sensitive toward themselves and others. The mistaking of sex and love is another example. The great power of sex (a physical act) lies inward in the capacity to love.

It seems to me religions make a profound error in this region. When a religion is born the leader and his immediate followers feel the truth opened. But generations later these truths are taught like canned answers to an exam. The student is looked upon dubiously if he doesn't take to the subject in this form. It would seem far more powerful an approach if religion opened up the feelings of individuals and then showed how these feelings were reflected in doctrine, ceremony, and tradition. Until religion can be lived, it has no life.

The simplest example of this inner/outer business is in books. The power of a book (an outer) lies in how well it effects the inner of persons. Mystics know that the sacred is automatically guarded by this means. How can anyone profane the Word, which merely sounds like ancient hogwash to them? The only one capable of profaning it is the one who feels its import. Insofar as one feels the import, he is less likely to profane it. It turns out that the sacred is naturally guarded by this means.

Through the whole descent a cardinal trend turns up. The inner will come out, will express itself. In fact, *what a person most essentially is, will be manifested.* This trend should be most apparent now. Everything inner touched upon—from reflecting on the self, to images, feelings, meditation, fringe phenomena, and dreams—has this self-representational trend. *The moment the mind gets away from its superficial activities and watches its inner tendencies it finds it is representing its own nature. This is the most fundamental, natural capacity of the mind.* Oddly enough I can't think of anyone who has said this except perhaps Swedenborg.

Whenever the person turns inward, the inner trends of the

person represent themself. In self-reflection this representation begins in what the individual feels of inner trends and values. The inner guides self-reflection. The representation gets more and more distinct in feeling/imagery, stilling the mind, fringe phenomena, and dreams. That limiting the operation of mind to focusing on a point intensifies its representational trend should be an apparent key. This is an underlying trend. The more the garbage of ego is shut off, the more intense the representation. It is like an underlying natural stream that can be covered over, but it cannot be stopped! The REM studies that experimentally try to stop dreaming indicate the power and importance of the dream. Stop dreaming for even five days, and the dream will break through and become hallucination. In psychotic hallucinations the impaired individual finds this inner representational trend spilling out into the world. My guess is that people with psychotic hallucinations have badly missed any capacity to live out their inner potentials. Just as stopping dreams makes them more powerful and apparent, not living out potentials makes them stand forth and appear as hallucinations. Hallucinations may be both more limited than the person and more gifted because this is the unconscious, unused potential of the person. I would not have guessed there would be a potential more limited than the person, but perhaps we are all potentially dumb and limited as well as potentially gifted. Much of the negative, lower-order hallucinations sound like a personified nagging conscience, unconscientiously running rampant.

I also would not have guessed that the death of self-awareness is the birth of the giant universal insight of satori. One would rather suspect that at the very bottom of mind there would be blank walls of nothingness instead of a breaking through to all else.

What Puzzles Remain?

The main, pervasive puzzle is why the inner is so thoroughly symbolic. I have often thought that if there were some wise figure residing in each person's head who wanted to illuminate the person, it would be most kind if he spoke ordinary language. Suppose the inner figure thought I should try to write a book. As soon as I fell asleep why not just say loud and clear, "You can write a book. You will have help. You just write a lot of little pages. They will make up the book you want." Instead the message came through in the form of a dream of making a mosaic of a sea wave, as described in the chapter on dreams. The same symbolizing tendency shows up all the way to the borders of ordinary conscious experience. But why? Does the dream process not care if it is understood? This doesn't seem to be true. It is consistently commenting on aspects of the individual's life. Looking over thousands of translated dreams, it appears that the dream maker's major concern is the quality and style of life of the individual. It cares. But not in our language.

We can work back from the evidence to guess at the nature of the source of the symbolism. We are going to try to figure the nature and life of the "one who represents" from its representations. It is guesswork, but educated from many effects of The Other Me. For ease of handling, let us call this one that represents at whatever level The Other Me.

The Other Me lives and does things. It exists in some kind of polar relationship to the ego. The more limited the ego's operations, the more intense are the effects of The Other Me. When the individual is within two minutes of death in anesthesia, The Other Me shows a power that looks to be cosmic in scope. The less ego, the more the work of The Other Me is apparent.

The Other Me seems to have a total intimacy with the life of the dreamer. It is partly this intimacy with the faintest fringes of associations and experiences of the dreamer that makes the language of the dream so subtle. It may speak of obvious aspects of the dreamer's life, but it does so using the richest base of memory, experience, associations, and feelings of the dreamer. We would have to say that The Other Me is profoundly intimate. This intimacy is so great as to give a blushingly revealing aspect to dreams. Everyone has dreams they would rather not announce to the world. This intimacy is partly blocked in hallucinations. It was mentioned how the hallucinations may have just certain senses or areas of memory to work through. We don't know why this is, but it may have to do with the general self-estrangement of the person with psychotic hallucinations. Even in hallucinations the intimacy is great enough. The young man with annoying female breasts didn't know his ambivalence about his girl friends was getting in the way until we worked out the meaning of the breasts. The Other Me is intimate enough that one could say he (she, it) resides at the very seat of government of the person. The Other Me is certainly in a key position.

The work of The Other Me seems to reflect a central concern with the quality of the individual's life. It is true that some fantasies or dreams merely serve to remind the person of minor trends already known to him. The Other Me can be light or playful like "The Emanation of Feminine Aspect of the Divine," who showed persons were right by handing over her panties. Yet if we reflect on the whole scope of the output of The Other Me, it seems to be gently leading the individual to understand his own nature, potential, and trends. Even the most limited and mean work of The Other Me, the lower order of hallucinations, serves to illustrate the faults of the person. When the alcoholic hears voices discussing how they should dispose of this rotten worthless bum, even here The Other Me seems concerned with the quality of the person's life. The Other Me is also relatively patient. No ordinary person could design thousands of clever dreams for an individual and watch them all go to waste.

The Other Me seems to know more than the individual, in fact a great deal more. Very ordinary dreams illustrate that the maker of the dream has more insight than the dreamer. This is another factor that contributes to the difficulty of understanding The Other Me's language. Little touches—like "abraxas" in my dream, ESP in hallucinations, and, above all, the giftedness of the higher order hallucinations—suggest that The Other Me has much more information than the dreamer. In fact, occasionally The Other Me looks like wisdom itself.

That's all very well, but why can't it speak ordinary language? It can but it doesn't do so often. It appears to understand language itself better than the individual as complex plays on words in dreams and hallucinations suggest. Ordinary language doesn't appear to be its easiest, or most natural mode. What is this symbolism or representational tendency? It is to portray what is psychical or spiritual in material terms. For instance, a dream will say you are deceptive by a little drama of someone stealing something. The Other Me is portraying things we have to talk about abstractly (i.e., one's nature, tendencies, potentials, etc.) in terms of real things. The Other Me is very much like the playwright who presents a complex human problem in terms of a drama. The Other Me must know both, inner trends and real life, to speak a language that fuses them together. In its writing of plays it varies over the whole scope of human drama from gross humor to the highest wisdom.

Let us summarize what we can guess of The Other Me to this point.

(a) It lives and does things.

(b) It exists in some kind of polar relationship to ego or self-awareness. The less self-awareness, the more the activity of

The Other Me becomes apparent.

(c) It has total intimacy with the individual.

(d) It has a central concern with the quality of the life.

(e) It knows far more than the individual. There are intimations that it knows more of history and may be able to see the future.

(f) It knows both the inner and outer realities and tends to treat these as one.

(g) Its natural mode is representation or symbolizing in which something higher or more inner is illustrated by a dramatic arrangement of elements from a lower level.

While we can be relatively sure representation or symbolizing is its natural mode, it is still not clear why it is. This problem occupied me for several years off and on. If we contrast our ordinary language of no symbols to a language that is all symbols we will see more clearly what The Other Me is. In the world of no symbols a house is simply a house, a tree is a tree. In the world of symbols a house is also one's abode, place in the world, style of living, the outer quality of one's being, etc. Its meaning is spread to all its possible implications. Our thinking normally approaches reality from the limited view of a house. The Other Me, whose natural mode is to think symbolically, tends to see all things as related. From The Other Me's viewpoint this, that, and the other are all aspects of each other. Symbolic thinking shows the internal connections in this world in which all things are related. *These inner processes of mind tend to be symbolic because they stem from a world in which all things are understood as related.* This is a higher and richer sort of thinking than we are accustomed to.

One might think that at least the life of the individual is a clearly demarked entity to The Other Me, yet this is not so either. When I dream of you, you are part of me. When you dream of me, I am part of you. In this inner world of symbols everything images everything else, which is a world of total consciousness. On all levels of this inward journey it is possible to break through into this total imaging, symbolizing, awareness, which is the root tendency of all inner processes. *This pervasive inner quality points toward a source that functions as though all things were related.* Hence we are puzzled by glimpses of this inner world and have to laboriously work out new connections and associations of ideas. The source of these images has no problem with seeing rich interconnections. It has to severely limit itself to think as simply as we do.

When we look inward at the natural consistency of the inner processes, we look toward a very intimate, very wise source that tends to see all things as related. Those who know anything of theology may see that we are pointing toward a source that is Godlike. Hence satori, brief periods of Godlike awareness, is possible. Yet the beauty and paradox of the whole situation deepens if we look from such a source back into our most ordinary kinds of experiencing. Again I draw on Swedenborg, the only mystic whose knowledge of all the lower levels of the psyche I can really respect.

Representations are nothing but images of spiritual things in natural ones, and when the former are rightly represented in the latter, then the two correspond. Yet the man who knows not what the Spiritual is, but only the Natural, is capable of thinking that such representations and derivative correspondences are impossible, for he might say to himself, how can what is spiritual act upon what is material? But if he will reflect upon the things taking place in himself in every moment, he may be able to gain some idea of these matters; for instance, how the will can act upon the muscles of the body, and effect real actions; also how thought can act upon the organs of speech, moving the lungs, trachea, throat, tongue and lips, and thus produce speech; and also how the affections can act on the face, and there present images of themselves, so that another often thereby knows what is being thought and felt. These examples may give some idea of what representations and correspondences are. As such things are now presented in man, and as there is nothing that can subsist from itself, but only from some other, and this again from some other, and finally from the First, and this by a connection of correspondences, those who enjoy any extension of judgment may draw the conclusion that there is a correspondence between man and heaven; and further, between heaven and The Lord who is The First [*Arcana Coelestia*, ¶ 4044].

The reason why all and each of those things which exist in the spiritual world has its representation in the natural world, is because what is internal takes to itself a suitable clothing in what is external, by means of which it renders itself visible and appears [from *The White Horse Mentioned in the Apocalypse*].

In other words, all the outer aspects of man are representations of the inner, and the inner through a series of correspondences is a representation of The One. Representation is the means by which something higher can be illustrated in things lower. It is a natural mode all the way from The One down through man. Thought and action itself are representative of what is inner.

Our whole lives and, indeed, our every action are the end point of a gigantic process of representations. And the world we experience is certainly a continuation of this representational process. We are a higher process manifesting itself in the limitations of our existence.

If you suppose that self-representation is part of a natural process that extends beyond man, the remaining problems are cleared up. The persistence and even intensifying of the representational process would be accounted for. It is not just an accident of sloppy thinking on the part of unconscious processes as some would suppose. It is part of the very nature of the inner aspect of man. If it is part of both the innermost processes of man and of creation beyond man, then the surprising findings of satori become conceivable. If man is part of a continuum extending beyond him, then occasional insights into the over-all nature of that continuum would be possible. Most of the continuum extends beyond time, so extrasensory perception is possible. The whole wisdom of internal symbols becomes more reasonable. It is also possible for this inner to know more than the individual has had access to, i.e., arcane references in dreams and in higher-order hallucinations.

A surprising possibility is that supposing man's innermost is part of this continuum makes possible the heaven and hell aspects of psychotic hallucinations. This matter is both too complex and too filled with uncertainties to make it convincing in a few words. It would require a whole volume in itself. But, as described by Swedenborg, heaven and hell are themselves part of this continuum of representations that extend beyond man. It is conceivable that psychotic hallucinations represent an unwanted breakthrough into other levels of existence.

In any event, The Other Me has to lie beyond the accepted bounds of the individual as he is ordinarily conceived. Either the conception of the limits of the person has to be greatly expanded or we have to concede that higher processes are reflected in us. In a real way it would be vain pretension to claim The Other Me as our own since he is known so little and we have no control over him. It would seem more modest and fitting to concede that higher processes are reflected in us.

There are several practical aspects to this representational language of The Other Me. It leaves the will of the individual relatively free. If voices told me to write a book I would feel more under obligation to do it than if they simply present an interesting little drama. Higher-order hallucinations are careful to leave the individual's will free. Those of the lower order are just the opposite. They are out to capture and control the person. It might be more accurate to say The Other Me leaves the person's will free until the individual fails to live out the inner trends. Then the inner trends can run over the individual in madness, in lesser psychopathology, and to a lesser extent in nightmares that leave a disturbing impression. We are freer the closer we come to our own natural tendencies. To depart from them damages freedom and can destroy it in madness.

Another practical aspect of this representational tendency is that one has to feel into the living basis of the symbol to read back its meaning. This is done in free-associating to dream elements. Like the natural barriers around the sacred, the representational language has this same natural barrier. To understand a thief in a dream, one needs to feel like a thief.

Summary

With a great deal of empirical evidence and a little supposing, it is possible now to roughly describe the design of the inner world.

Its most pervasive aspect is that it naturally, easily, and consistently tends to reveal the inner dispositions, tendencies, and values of the individual. This begins in the simplest processes of self-reflection, intensifies in exercises that allow the projection of meaning, and deepens even further in the stilling of ego. The process becomes quite clear in dreams. When the individual's potentials are not lived out it can break through into normal waking life as in hallucinations. The process is intrinsically wise and can lead and educate the individual if its guidance is understood and followed.

It is as though the person were given ample clues as to his nature and the over-all direction of his life. *Very clearly man's mind is fundamentally designed as a self-informing, self-guiding system.*

The main problem is that the inner is higher than the individual. The innermost is a region that seems to understand all things as interrelated. Several puzzles are solved if this inner language is supposed to reflect a general process by which The One forms creation as successive levels of representation of

Itself. It would account both for the existence of satori and the relatively universal insights gained by it. It would account for the richness and wisdom of the inner. In a profound way it is fortunate that the individual needs to be in the spirit of the inner to understand its language. We must become inner to understand the inner. It is fortunate that the inner cannot be violated by our manipulations. Apparently it will live and will express its guiding wisdom whether or not the individual cares or understands. It is like a subtle potential that requires the deepending of humanness even to approach and understand it. Should the individual miss the fulfilling of his nature, the inner will stand forth nevertheless as feelings, guilt, images, fantasies, dreams, and if need be will become visible and heard. Apparently we have ample guidance to become what we essentially are. If we miss our nature, its warning signs become louder and clearer. The real surprise is the strangely transcendent language of the inner. But then it is good that the language itself requires deepening of humanness to understand it—a wise and unexpected kind of guide. And of course the inner processes are very patient. The puzzle of humanness is apparently not meant to be a simple affair to be easily mastered. Whatever deals with human lives is naturally patient.

It is beyond the scope of the matters presented here, but the journey inward into depth is a long, complex deepening of the implications of humanness. The personal identity and history on the superficial level of consciousness deepen into the innate, natural tendencies. It is as though in the depth is the main part of ourselves and the depth leads the individual *through* the circumstances of his life *along* the lines of his innate tendencies. This is the Way for the individual. The felt freedom of the indiviudal increases along this Way. The possible dramas include all human dramas, and especially all those needed by the individual to perfect him. The simple bounds of self are broken open to include all selves, under all circumstances, through all time. Indeed, the bounds break open beyond humanness to include all life and even the material world.

In the natural depth of man is a transcendent process that can guide and educate the individual. It is heartening to see something of the pattern of wisdom that is all ourselves.

Appendix
The Life of Emanuel Swedenborg

So many references have been made to Emanuel Swedenborg and so few know of the man that there may be interest in learning of his extraordinary life. He was born in 1688, the son of a devout bishop in Sweden who served the king. Early in his life the family was ennobled, which changed the name from Swedberg to Swedenborg. Emanuel had the customary classical education, with a heavy emphasis on Greek and Latin.

Early in life he was disappointed in a love affair and never married. It was as though all his energy and passion was turned to mastering knowledge. He may have been the last man to have encompassed all that was known. He worked as assessor of mines for Sweden. In this position he traveled all over Europe and brought back new ideas on mining, thereby enriching Sweden. He was interested in practically everything. Up to the age of sixty-one he wrote 154 works in some seventeen sciences, several of which he founded. Though he was later to be known as a mystic, there is no question that he was a master of sciences. It was his habit to learn all there was in a given field, write on it, and then go to another area. To give some idea of his range of areas, they include soils and muds, stereometry, echoes, algebra and calculus, blast furnaces, astronomy, economics, magnetism, and hydrostatics. He was the first to formulate the nebular hypothesis of the creation of the universe. His works in human anatomy alone would satisfy most men as an adequate lifetime accomplishment. He was the first to discover the functions of the ductless glands and the cerebellum.

In addition to mastering nine languages, Swedenborg was an inventor and a craftsman. His inventions include a submarine, air pumps, musical instruments, a glider, and mining equipment. He helped engineer the world's largest drydock and once got a ship over a mountain. To pass the time he enjoyed moving in with craftsmen and learning their trade. It appears that he mastered at least seven crafts. He made his own scientific instruments including a microscope. In addition, he was a musician and a respected member of the Swedish parliament.

Had he stopped with these minor accomplishments he would have been remembered as a great scientist. But late in life he went on to other discoveries that were so incredible that they cast a shadow over his name, so much so that many now forget his scientific mastery. In his late fifties he took on the mind as his next area. By this time his income was such that he no longer needed to work. He took on psychology with his usual thoroughness. As a starter he surveyed all that was known of the mind and published this in several volumes, together with some observations of his own. He was really trying to reach and understand the soul.

He started writing down and interpreting his own dreams. His understanding of the structure of dream language two centuries ago is about what ours is today. Since childhood Swedenborg had practised a way of suspending breathing and drawing his attention inward in what looks like Raja Yoga practice. He followed this way of intensifying inner processes. Very soon he was watching the symbol making inner processes. He did the most detailed and revealing study of the hypnogogic state ever done before or since. Yet this was just the beginning of his search. He began to pick up the presence of other beings in this inner state, something that those who study the hypnogogic can relatively easily duplicate. Finally inner processes were intensified until he could walk around in and fully experience heaven and hell while living a normal life. In his usual scientific way he carefully recorded all this in his five-volume *Spiritual Diary* and other volumes. The *Diary* was the notes of a great explorer. It was not meant for others to see. It is curious to see in his dreams this great man wrestling with his own normal sexual needs. He had a profound respect for women and marriage that culminated at the age of eighty in his beautiful volume *Conjugial Love*.

It is fascinating to compare his writings before and after this long period of inner exploration. The work that came before was terribly intellectual and colored with natural pride in his accomplishments. Yet the intellect was always searching for the truth. There is a sudden and dramatic change in his works beginning with the twelve-volume *Arcana Coelestia* at age sixty-one. Pride was gone. His greatest theological works appeared without his name on them. There was no longer the searching. He was speaking of the most far-reaching spiritual/psychological matters with complete certainty. The brilliant intellect had become very much tempered with feeling. It was clear now that feeling was seen as greater than intellect. He now showed a complete familiarity with symbolism. Swedenborg had changed completely.

From the age of fifty-seven until his death at eighty-four he wrote some 282 works beyond the prior 155 in science. These were written in Latin, the universal language of his day. He published just the best of these at his own expense to be sold at near cost. These anonymous psychological/spiritual works were sent to the leading bishops and thinkers of his day but received little notice. They gradually caught the interest of more common people. He had found too much to be readily accepted or appreciated then or now.

While enjoying the freedom of heaven and hell he lived a normal life. He retired to a garden cottage in London and lived a very simple life of plain meals and a heavy routine of writing broken only by business trips abroad or royal gatherings. Contemporary observers described him as a modest, friendly man with a slight hesitancy in his speech. His was a life of observing and writing to give his findings to others.

It gradually became known that Swedenborg was the author of these extraordinary works. Because he was far beyond the religious teachings of his day (and, indeed, of today), he was tried as a heretic in Sweden and for many years his works were banned there. Rumors circulated that he was mad. He found too much, described too much. His reputation as a great scientist was overshadowed by his psychological/religious findings. An incident will illustrate this. His servants came to him saying they thought they should leave his employ because there was so much talk that he was not godly. Swedenborg answered simply that they knew his private life in all its aspects. If they could think of any single incident in which he acted un-Christian in their eyes, they were free to go. They stayed. Very understanding friends asked him to at least go to church. He probably found church a bit boring, but to set a good example for others he went anyway.

Swedenborg answered freely any honest questions directed to him about the spiritual world. He must have been something of a conversation stopper when he spoke of his most recent experiences in the spiritual world at a party. Once a group of men joshed him and asked if he could tell who was to die next. Without hesitating Swedenborg said that yes, Mr. so-and-so, who lived nearby, was to die at 2 A.M. the next morning. And he did. The Queen of Sweden asked him to get in touch with a deceased brother. The next day when he reported back she fainted dead away. He revealed what only she and the brother knew. The most famous miracle occurred at a party. He became visibly disturbed. When asked what was wrong, he said that Stockholm was burning. He described the fire in detail. It quit near his home. A couple of days later his report was confirmed. There were many parallel incidents in which Swedenborg put no stock at all. He didn't bother to write these down, but others did.

The most impressive incident occurred in conjunction with John Wesley, the founder of Methdodism, and is described in Wesley's writings. Swedenborg wrote to Wesley saying that he had learned in heaven that Wesley wanted to meet with him. Wesley was a little surprised. He said that it was true, and could they get together on a given date. Swedenborg wrote a note of apology. He couldn't meet on that date because he was due to die on a given date, which he did. There were many signs that he was in touch with worlds beyond this one, but he considered this unimportant. The man who really wanted to know the truth would be able to discern it in his many writings.

Several aspects of Swedenborg's works interst me. He was an early phenomenologist. Though the mode of approach in his day to psychology was philosophical speculation, he was basically an observer of experience. He explored the inward realm perhaps more than anyone else in the Western world. His works cross the psychological/spiritual boundary with the ease of one accustomed to the interrelationship of these realms. And the richness of his works is sufficient to occupy one for a lifetime. The symbolism of inner states and the Bible becomes very clear and very human. And by minor exploration the reader can find a similar language in himself.

But relatively few are captivated by his works. There is a handful of followers in various lands. Perhaps it is necessary to have personally explored psychological/spiritual states to appreciate the richness of his works.

There are several biographies, but the best of these is by George Trobridge, *Swedenborg, Life and Teaching*. One of the best studies of his thought is John Spaulding, *Introduction to Sedenborg's Religious Thought*. His most popular writings and an appropriate place to begin study are *Heaven and Hell, Divine Love and Wisdom,* or *Divine Providence. Arcana Coelestia* is more appropriate for advanced scholars, unless one has a particular interest in biblical symbolism. His writings are available in most public libraries or at cost from:

The Swedenborg Foundation, 139 East 23rd Street, New York, N.Y. 10010;

The Swedenborg Society, 20 Bloomsbury Way, London W.C. 1A, England;

Swedenborg Verlag, Apollostrasse 2, 8032, Zurich, Switzerland;

Swedenborg Publisher, 136 Onuma-cho, Kodaira-shi, Tokyo, Japan.

References

CHAPTER—3

1. R. Sommer, *Personal Space* (New York: Prentice-Hall, 1969).
2. K. Machover, *Personality Projection in the Drawing of the Human Figure* (Springfield, Ill.: C. C. Thomas, 1949).
3. M. L. Hutt and G. J. Briskin, *The Clinical Use of the Revised Bender Gestalt Test* (New York: Grune and Stratton, 1960).
4. J. H. Van den Berg, *The Phenomenological Approach to Psychiatry* (Springfield, Ill.: C. C. Thomas, 1955).
   L. Binswanger, *Being in the World* (New York: Basic Books, 1963).
5. A. Lowen, *Physical Dynamics of Character Structure* (New York: Grune and Stratton, 1958).
6. C. Man-ch'ing and R. Smith, *Tai Chi* (Rutland, Vt.: C. E. Tuttle, 1967).

CHAPTER—4

1. Gabriel Marcel, *The Philosophy of Existence* (London: Harvill Press, 1948).
2. Marcel, *Metaphysical Journal* (London: Rockliff, 1952).

Chapter—6

1. C. Brownfield, *Isolation* (New York: Random House, 1965).
2. I. Oswald, *Sleeping and Waking* (New York: Elsevier, 1962).
3. William James, *The Varieties of Religious Experience* (New York: Modern Library, 1902), see pp. 378 f. In this experiment I was repeating the work of William James and Benjamin Blood and had similar experiences.
4. I. Deva, *Yoga for Americans* (Englewood Cliffs, N. J.: Prentice-Hall, 1959).
5. R. Bucke, *Cosmic Consciousness* (New York: Dutton, 1901). Wilson Van Dusen, "LSD and the Enlightenment of Zen," *Psychologia* 4 (1961): 11–16.

Chapter—7

1. By Emanuel Swedenborg:
   Journal of Dreams (Bryn Athyn, Pa: Academy Book Room, 1918). This volume is very rare.
   The Spiritual Diary, 5 vols. (London: Swedenborg Society, 1962); originally written in 1748–1767.
2. Swedenborg, *Arcana Coelestia*, 12 vols. (New York: Swedenborg Foundation, 1960).
   G. Trobridge, *Swedenborg, Life and Teaching* (London: Swedenborg Society, 1945); about the best biography of Swedenborg's impressive life.
3. Swedenborg, *Heaven and Hell* (New York: Swedenborg Foundation, 1960).
4. Jean-Paul Sartre, *The Psychology of Imagination* (New York: Citadel Press, 1961).
5. Herbert Silberer, "Report on a Method of Eliciting and Observing Certain Symbolic Hallucination Phenomena," in D. Rapaport, *Organization and Pathology of Thought* (New York: Columbia University Press, 1951).

6. I. Oswald, *Sleeping and Waking* (New York: Elsevier, 1962), see pp. 96 f.

7. Carl Jung, *The Collected Works of Carl Jung* (New York: Pantheon Books).

CHAPTER—8

1. I. Oswald, *Sleeping and Waking* (New York: Elsevier, 1962).
   M. Kramer, *Dream Psychology and the New Biology of Dreaming* (Springfield, Ill.: C. C. Thomas, 1969).
   L. Caligor and Rollo May, *Dream Symbols, Man's Unconscious Language* (New York: Basic Books, 1970).
   E. Gutheil, *What Your Dreams Mean* (Greenwich, Conn.: Premier, 1957).
   C. Hall, *The Meaning of Dreams* (New York: Modern Library, 1950).

2. Sigmund Freud, *The Interpretation of Dreams* (New York: Modern Library, 1950).

3. Fritz Perls, *Gestalt Therapy Verbatim* (Moab, Utah: Real People Press, 1969).

4. H. Shevrin and L. Luborsky, "The Measurement of Preconscious Perception in Dreams and Images: An Investigation of the Poetzl Phenomenon," *Journal of Abnormal and Social Psychology* 56 (1958): 285 f.

5. E. Aserinsky and N. Kleitman, "Two Types of Ocular Motility Occurring in Sleep," *Journal of Applied Physiology* 8 (1955): 1–10.

6. Wilson Van Dusen, *Mind in Hyperspace* (Ann Arbor: University Microfilms, No. 59–849, 1959).

7. *Encyclopaedia Britannica* (Chicago: William Benton, 1966), vol. 1, p. 47.

Chapter—9

1. Wilson Van Dusen, "The Psychologist's Role in the Therapeutic Community," *The California State Psychologist* 1, no. 3 (1959): 7–8.

   Van Dusen, "A Central Dynamism in Chronic Schizophrenia," *Psychoanalysis and the Psychoanalytic Review* 46 (1959): 85–91.

   Van Dusen, "The Phenomenology of a Schizophrenic Existence," *Journal of Individual Psychology* 17 (1961): 80–92.

   Wilson Van Dusen, Ernest Klatte, and Wayne Wilson, "Non Medical Unit Administration," *Mental Hospitals* 14 (1963): 483–86.

   Wilson Van Dusen, Homer Mathews, Dixie Quinlan, and B. Galbraith, "Characteristics of an Aged State Hospital Population," *California Mental Health Research Digest* 1 (1964): 15–16.

   Wilson Van Dusen, Wayne Wilson, William Miners, and Harry Hook, "Treatment of Alcoholism with Lysergide," *Quarterly Journal of Studies of Alcohol* 28 (1967): 295–304. Lysergide is the drug LSD.

   Wilson Van Dusen, Rudi Holzinger, and R. Mortimer, "Aversion Conditioning Treatment of Alcoholism," *American Journal of Psychiatry* 124 (1967): 246–47.

   Van Dusen, "Capacities of the Aged Chronic Mentally Ill," *California Mental Health Research Digest*, Summer (1968): 136–37.

   Wilson Van Dusen and Bryce Brooks, "Treatment of Youthful Drug Abusers," *Modern Medicine* (July 27, 1970): 74–76.

2. Thomas Szasz, *The Myth of Mental Illness* (New York: Hoeber-Harper, 1961).

3. M. Sechehaye, *The Autobiography of a Schizophrenic Girl* (New York: Grune and Stratton, 1951).

4. Emanuel Swedenborg, *On the Divine Love and on the Divine Wisdom* (New York: Swedenborg Foundation, 1965; formerly published under the title *Doctrine of Uses*).

5. Maxwell Jones, *Therapeutic Community* (New York: Basic Books, 1953).

Jones, *Beyond the Therapeutic Community* (New Haven: Yale University Press, 1968).

6. D. L. Briggs, "Convicted Felons as Social Therapists," *Correctional Psychiatry and Journal of Social Therapy* 9 (1963): 122–26.

CHAPTER—10

1. By Wilson Van Dusen:
   The Presence of Spirits in Madness (New York: Swedenborg Foundation, 1968). "Confronting Hallucinations," two hours of recording on tape (Big Sur, Calif.: Esalen Foundation, 1969). *Die Gegenwart von Geistern im Wahnsinn* (Zurich: Swedenborg Verlag, 1967).
   "Hallucinations as the World of Spirits," *Psychedelic Review* 11 (1971): 60–69.
2. Emanuel Swedenborg, *Heaven and Hell* (New York: Swedenborg Foundation, 1970); also see his 5-volume *Spiritual Diary*.
3. Van Dusen, op. cit.

CHAPTER—11

1. Wilson Van Dusen, "LSD and the Enlightenment of Zen," *Psychologia* 4 (1961): 11–16. This was later translated into Japanese and published in a Zen Buddhist journal *Daihorin* (The Great Dharma Wheel), October 1961: 146–53.
   Van Dusen, "Second Epistle to the Romans," *Psychedelic Review* 6 (1965): 98–103.
2. William James, *The Varieties of Religious Experience* (New York; Modern Library, 1902).
   R. Bucke, *Cosmic Consciousness* (New York: Dutton, 1901).
3. There are many translations of the *Bhagavad Gita*. It is the Hindu's most popular book of devotions from the ancient Mahabharata.
4. Emanuel Swedenborg, *Arcana Coelestia*, 12 vols. (New York: Swedenborg Foundation, 1950).